GREATEST INSPIRATIONAL QUOTES

1000

DAYS OF INSPIRING QUOTES AND CONTEMPLATIONS TO DISCOVER YOUR INNER STRENGTH AND TRANSFORM YOUR LIFE

ALBERT GOODMAN

Albert Goodman has asserted his moral right to be identified as the author of this work in accordance with the Copyright, Designs and Patents Act 1988

Copyright © 2019 Albert Goodman

All rights reserved

DEDICATION

*I dedicate this book to all my teachers,
past and future.*

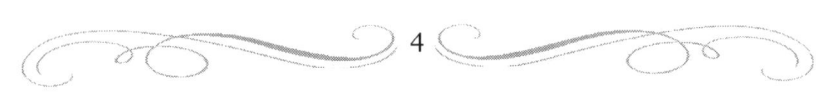

TABLE OF CONTENTS

Introduction 6
George Washington 11
Richard Branson 12
Napoleon Hill 16
Benjamin Franklin 19
Abraham Lincoln 21
Oprah Winfrey 24
Sophie Kinsella 33
Harriet Tubman 36
Warren Edward Buffett 41
John D. Rockefeller 44
Steve Jobs 47
Bill Gates 52
Katherine Mansfield 54
Elon Musk 59
Elizabeth Taylor 62
Jim Rohn 69
Dale Carnegie 72
Bodo Schafer 75
Thomas Edison 76
Albert Einstein 79
Princess Diana 82
Robert Kiyosaki 86
Thomas More 90
Nancy Astor 92
Ferdinand Porsche 96
Margaret Thatcher 97
Winston Churchill 101

- Bruce Lee 102
- Sophia Loren 105
- Mike Tyson 111
- Muhammad Ali 113
- Joan Crawford 114
- Amelia Earhart 119
- Will Smith 123
- John C. Maxwell 128
- Napoleon Bonaparte 133
- Confucius 135
- Sun Tzu 138
- Genghis Khan 140
- Gaius Julius Caesar 142
- Anna Eleanor Roosevelt 145
- John Kennedy 161
- Connie Podesta 164
- Alexander The Great 170
- Hillary Clinton 172
- Julia Child 175
- Lao Tzu 183
- Elizabeth Arden 185
- Gloria Steinem 200
- Henry Ford 211
- Sally Kristen Ride 214
- Oscar Wilde 218
- Joan Rivers 220

INTRODUCTION

It is no myth that words have power. It's almost baffling how a carefully selected group of words have the ability to influence one's life and decisions. A set of words should be able to influence your life positively for it to be termed as inspirational. It is safe to say that we all need a bit of inspiration in life. Some of us more than others, but a quote a day can go a long way in shaping one's destiny.

The goal of this book is to give the reader a good start to any day. It contains the very best of inspirational quotes, carefully selected to give you that extra boost you need every day. Not only do you get that inspirational quote in this book, but you will also get to learn the in-depth meaning of each quote and how you can relate to it.

We often look for inspiration in all the wrong places; yet, inspiration lies within us. In this book, you will discover the potential that lies within you. You will finally understand how you are your *own* motivation. You will develop courage to face every challenge that comes your way.

Truly understanding one's self is the beginning of realizing potential. Once you realize your potential, it will be difficult for anything to hold you back. These quotes encourage you to see the greatness that is within you and guide you in unlocking your potential.

Reading this book is a journey of self-discovery. In this journey, you will be able to comprehend how to influence those around you to recognize the internal motivation they need. This book is for everyone, regardless of age, gender, career, position, or any other aspect of life.

Self-discovery is optional. Not many seek it, but we all need it. When you picture all the things you could achieve upon finding your true purpose in life, you will find that self-discovery is an inevitable journey for us all. The words of this book are just the initial stepping stones of your journey.

For a leader or anyone tasked with a presentation of any kind, this book can come in handy in all stages of your presentation. Starting from preparation, to rehearsal, and finally on stage, you will be able to meaningfully connect with your audience and bring them to an understanding of your material.

If you are a boss, you probably know that your team looks up to you for guidance. Now picture yourself being an inspirational boss so that, whenever you talk, your crew feels so motivated that they produce results beyond your expectations. Use the inspiration you receive from this book and gift it to others.

I am so certain you will find this book uplifting that you will find yourself giving this book as a gift to all the important people in your life. Since the pages contain quotes for each day of the year, they will never run out of inspirational quotes. Inspiration is a timeless gift one can use for a lifetime.

How to use this book

The inspirational quotes in this book have a specific purpose for your life; therefore, it is imperative that you make it a point to read at least one quote each day. All provided quotes have different impacts. There is always a quote that directly relates to your current situation.

Below is a simple guide on how to utilize this book to its full potential:

1. **Maximize the book's content**

This simply means that you ensure you have read each of the quotes within the book. This does not mean that one reads the whole book in one day.

For maximum utility of this book, you can decide to either be reading one quote a day or a few quotes a day. In so doing, the effectiveness of the quotes will definitely be visible in your life.

2. **Be inspired daily**

The capacity of quality inspirational quotes in this book is enough to cover a whole year and more than a third of the second year if used daily.

Make it a daily routine that you infuse your mornings with at least one inspirational quote. It does not have to be in the order they are written; you may select a random quote and use it to get the inspiration that you need each day.

3. **Consistency is key**

We all desire long term results as the effects are long lasting. For you to get long term results, you will have to be disciplined enough that no morning goes by without you reading a quote from this book.

Adopt it as a lifestyle and live it like you mean it. The eventual results are effective no matter your position or lifestyle.

4. **Relate**

Having the ability to relate the passages within is a very important aspect of reading this book. You should take your time and internalize each quote. Afterwards, you should be able to identify how each quote fits into your current situation, or your life in general. Finding the point of connection between the quote and your life is the best way to get the most out of the inspiration offered.

5. **Challenge yourself**

Some quotes in this book are aimed at ensuring that you soar to new heights and attain what are deemed to be unreachable goals. Once you get to such a quote, the ideal way to go about it is to challenge yourself by breaking the bigger target into smaller, manageable targets; after all, *it is better to try and fail than fail to try.*

Important things to note

It is important that the reader understands that the quotes contained in this book have original authors and as such, are not the works of the author of this book. The author of this book provides guidance to the reader in regards to the selected quotes that appear in this book.

Every quote written in this book is applicable to all regardless of the gender, age, or any other factor indicated on any given quote. The reader should not dismiss any quote on the grounds of gender sensitivity, age restriction, social status, etc.

While sharing any quote from this book, please refer to the original author provided and not to the author of this book.

The reader should note that some quotes hold a deeper meaning rather than the surface meaning:

"I can't change the direction of the wind, but I can adjust my sails to always reach my destination."

Always remember to ruminate and internalize the deepest possible meaning of every quote. This will maximize your inspiration and move you to action.

GEORGE WASHINGTON

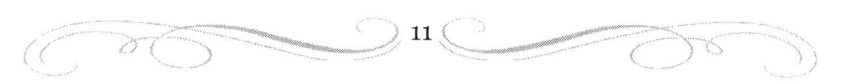

George Washington (February 22, 1732 – December 14, 1799) was an American politician and soldier who served as the first President of the United States.

* * *

Leave nothing for tomorrow which can be done today.

* * *

Associate with men of good quality if you esteem your own reputation.

* * *

There is nothing which can better deserve your patronage, than the promotion of science and literature. Knowledge is in every country the surest basis of public happiness.

* * *

Happiness and moral duty are inseparably connected.

* * *

Be courteous to all, but intimate with few, and let those few be well tried before you give them your confidence.

* * *

It is better to offer no excuse
than a bad one.

* * *

Liberty, when it begins to take root,
is a plant of rapid growth.

RICHARD BRANSON

Richard Branson (born 18 July 1950) - is an English business magnate, investor, and philanthropist. He founded the Virgin Group, which controls more than 400 companies.

* * *

Respect is how to treat everyone,
not just those you want to impress.

* * *

Building a business is not rocket science,
it's about having a great idea
and seeing it through with integrity.

* * *

Screw it. Let's do it.

* * *

Learn from failure.
If you are an entrepreneur
and your first venture wasn't a success,
welcome to the club!

* * *

My definition of success?
The more you're actively and practically engaged,
the more successful you will feel.

* * *

Happiness is the secret ingredient for successful businesses.
If you have a happy company
it will be invincible.

* * *

There is no greater thing you can do with your life
and your work than follow your passions –
in a way that serves the world and you.

* * *

Whatever business you are in,
every company can shoot for the start
in their own way.

* * *

When you're first thinking through an idea,
it's important not to get bogged down in complexity.
Thinking simply and clearly is hard to do.

* * *

If you don't have time for the small things,
you won't have time for the big things.

* * *

Communication - the thing humans forgot
when we invented words.

* * *

Listen.
Take the best.
Leave the rest.

* * *

Entrepreneurial business favors the open mind.
It favors people whose optimism drives them

to prepare for many possible futures,
pretty much purely for the joy of doing so.

* * *

If you spot an opportunity and are really excited by it, throw
yourself into it with everything you've got.

* * *

Engage your emotions at work.
Your instincts and emotions are there to help you.

* * *

Do not be embarrassed by your failures,
learn from them and start again.

* * *

You've got to take risks if you're going to succeed.
I would much rather ask forgiveness than permission.

* * *

Take a chance.
It's the best way to test yourself.
Have fun and push boundaries.

NAPOLEON HILL

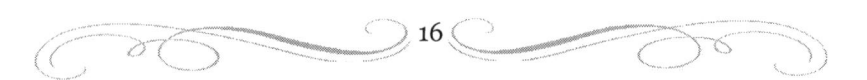

Napoleon Hill (October 26, 1883 – November 8, 1970) - was an American author and speaker. Hill is well known for his book "Think and Grow Rich."

* * *

If you do not see great riches in your imagination,
you will never see them in your bank balance

* * *

Our minds become magnetized with the dominating thoughts we hold in our minds
and these magnets attract to us the forces, the people, the circumstances of life which harmonize with the nature of our dominating thoughts.

* * *

Mind control is the result of self-discipline and habit. You either control your mind, or it controls you.
There is no half-way compromise.

* * *

You are the master of your destiny. You can influence, direct
and control your own environment.
You can make your life what you want it to be.

* * *

Failure is a trickster with a keen sense of irony and cunning.
It takes great delight in tripping one
when success is almost within reach.

* * *

All achievement, all earned riches,
have their beginning in an idea!

* * *

When defeat comes, accept it as a signal
that your plans are not sound, rebuild those plans, and set
sail once more toward your coveted goal.

* * *

Fears are nothing more
than a state of mind.

* * *

Love is, without question,
life's greatest experience.

* * *

Set your mind on a definite goal
and observe how quickly the world stands aside
to let you pass.

* * *

Fear, the worst of all enemies, can be effectively cured by
forced repetition of acts of courage.

* * *

The way of success is the way of continuous
pursuit of knowledge.

BENJAMIN FRANKLIN

Benjamin Franklin (January 17, 1706 – April 17, 1790) was one of the Founding Fathers of the United States.

* * *

Well done is better than well said.

* * *

When you are finished changing,
you're finished.

* * *

Those things that hurt, instruct.

* * *

Many people die at twenty-five
and aren't buried until they are seventy-five.

* * *

Never ruin an apology
with an excuse.

* * *

Eat to live,
don't live to eat.

* * *

Well done is better
than well said.

* * *

Never confuse Motion with Action.

* * *

A good example is
the best sermon.

* * *

One today is worth two tomorrows.

* * *

Motivation is when your dreams put on work clothes.

* * *

You may delay, but time will not.

* * *

If you fail to plan,
you are planning to fail!

* * *

He that can have patience
can have what he will.

ABRAHAM LINCOLN

Abraham Lincoln (February 12, 1809– April 15, 1865) - the 16th President of The United States of American, politician, and lawyer.

* * *

And in the end, it is not the years in your life that count, it's the life in your years.

* * *

When I do good, I feel good.
When I do bad, I feel bad.
That's my religion.

* * *

I am a slow walker, but I never walk back.

* * *

Be sure you put your feet in the right place,
then stand firm.

* * *

Folks are usually about as happy as
they make their minds up to be.

* * *

Nearly all men can stand adversity,
but if you want to test a man's character,
give him power.

* * *

Those who deny freedom to others,
deserve it not for themselves.

* * *

There are no bad pictures;
that's just how your face looks sometimes.

* * *

If I were two-faced,
would I be wearing this one?

* * *

Do I not destroy my enemies
when I make them my friends?

* * *

My concern is not whether God is on our side;
my greatest concern is to be on God's side,
for God is always right.

* * *

We can complain because rose bushes have thorns,
or rejoice because thorn bushes have roses.

* * *

You can fool some of the people all of the time,
and all of the people some of the time,
but you cannot fool all of the people all of the time.

* * *

I am not bound to win, but I am bound to be true.
I am not bound to succeed,
but I am bound to live up to what light I have.

OPRAH WINFREY

Oprah Winfrey (born January 29, 1954) is an American media executive, actress, talk show host, television producer, and philanthropist. She is best known for her talk show The Oprah Winfrey Show, which was the highest-rated television program of its kind in history and was nationally syndicated from 1986 to 2011 in Chicago.

* * *

Don't worry about being successful but work toward being significant and the success will naturally follow.

* * *

Surround yourself only with people who are going to take you higher.

* * *

You can have it all. Just not all at once.

* * *

Turn your wounds into wisdom.

* * *

Where there is no struggle, there is no strength.

* * *

Do the one thing you think you cannot do. Fail at it. Try again. Do better the second time. The only people who never tumble are those who never mount the high wire. This is your moment. Own it.

* * *

We can't become what we need to be by remaining what we are.

* * *

As you become more clear about who you really are, you'll be better able to decide what is best for you – the first time around.

* * *

The more you praise and celebrate your life, the more there is in life to celebrate.

* * *

Listen to the rhythm of your own calling, and follow that.

* * *

Be thankful for what you have; you'll end up having more. If you concentrate on what you don't have, you will never have enough

* * *

The greatest discovery of all time is that a person can change their future by merely changing their attitude.

* * *

You become what you believe.

* * *

I don't think of myself as a poor deprived ghetto girl who made good. I think of myself as somebody who, from an early age, knew I was responsible for myself, and I had to make good.

* * *

Use your life to serve the world, and you will find that also serves you.

* * *

Failure is a great teacher. If you're open to it, every mistake has a lesson to offer.

* * *

What I know is that if you do work that you love, and the work fulfills you, the rest will come.

* * *

You can have it all. Just not at once.

* * *

Luck is a matter of preparation meeting opportunity.

* * *

Go ahead, fall down. The world looks different from the ground.

* * *

All my life I have wanted to lead people an empathy space. To a gratitude space. I want us all to fulfill our greatest potential. To find our calling, and summon the courage to live it.

* * *

You know you are on the road to success if you would do your job, and not be paid for it.

* * *

Failing is another stepping stone to greatness.

* * *

Follow your instincts. That is where true wisdom manifests itself.

You cannot hate other people without hating yourself.

* * *

The biggest adventure you can ever take is to live the life of your dreams.

* * *

The big secret in life is there is no secret. Whatever your goal. You can get there if you're willing to work.

* * *

Whatever you fear the most has no power, it is your fear that has no power. Oprah Winfrey

* * *

Create the highest grandest vision for your life. Then let every step move you in that direction.

* * *

The way through the challenge is to get still, and ask yourself: What is the next right move?

* * *

The truth is I have from the very beginning listened to my instincts. All of my best decisions in life have come because I was attuned to what really felt like the next right move for me. Oprah Winfrey

* * *

I don't believe in failure. Failure is just information and an opportunity to change your course.

* * *

You get in life what you have the courage to ask for.

* * *

There is a flow with your name on it. your job is to find it and let it carry you to the next level.

* * *

Doing the best at this moment puts you in the best place for the next moment.

* * *

The smallest change in perspective can transform a life. What tiny attitude adjustment might turn your world around.

* * *

The single greatest thing you can do to change your life today would be to start being grateful for what you have right now.

* * *

Trust that everything happens for a reason, even when you're not wise enough to see it.

* * *

Don't settle for a relationship that won't let you be yourself.

* * *

No experience is ever wasted. Everything has meaning.

* * *

The choice to be excellent begins with aligning your thoughts and words with the intention to require more from yourself.

* * *

Often, we don't even realize who we're meant to be because we're so busy trying to live out someone else's ideas. But other people and their opinions hold no power in defining our destiny.

* * *

Passion is energy. Feel the power that comes from focusing on what excites you.

* * *

With every experience, you alone are painting your own canvas, thought by thought, choice by choice.

* * *

I believe that one of life's greatest risks is never daring to risk.

* * *

What material success does is provide you with the ability to concentrate on other things that really matter. And that is being able to make a difference, not only in your own life but in other people's lives.

* * *

I know for sure that what we dwell on is who we become.

* * *

I had no idea that being your authentic self could make me as rich as I've become. If I had, I'd have done it a lot earlier.

* * *

Every time you state what you want or believe, you're the first to hear it. It's a message to both you and others about what you think is possible. Don't put a ceiling on yourself.

* * *

Your true passion should feel like breathing; it's that natural.

* * *

You have to know what sparks the light in you so that you, in your own way, can illuminate the world.

SOPHIE KINSELLA

Madeleine Sophie Wickham also known under the pen name Sophie Kinsella (born 12 December 1969) is an English author of chick lit.

* * *

There's no luck in business. There's only drive, determination, and more drive.

* * *

Darling, when things go wrong in life, you lift your chin, put on a ravishing smile, mix yourself a little cocktail…

* * *

I love new clothes. If everyone could just wear new clothes every day, I reckon depression wouldn't exist anymore.

* * *

Sometimes you don't need a goal in life, you don't need to know the big picture.

You just need to know what you're going to do next!

* * *

No human on God's earth is a nobody.

* * *

If you can't be honest with your friends and colleagues and loved ones, then what is life all about?

* * *

Life would be a lot easier if conversations were rewindable and erasable, like videos. Or if you could instruct people to disregard what you just said, like in a courtroom.

* * *

Still, that's the point of love – you love someone despite their flaws.

* * *

Some things are best left a blur. Births and Visa bills.

* * *

A man will never love you or treat you as well as a store. If a man doesn't fit, you can't exchange him seven days later for a gorgeous cashmere sweater. And a store always smells good. A store can awaken a lust for things you never even knew you needed. And when your fingers first grasp those shiny new bags...

* * *

Never give up on something you really want. However impossible things seem, there's always a way.

* * *

The thing with giving up is you never know. You never know whether you could have done the job. And I'm sick of not knowing about my life.

* * *

Everyone knows revenge is a dish best served when you've had enough time to build up enough vitriol and fury.

* * *

I'm Cinderella. No, I'm better than Cinderella, because she only got the prince, didn't she? I'm Cinderella with fab teeth and a shit-hot job.

* * *

People who want to make a million borrow a million first.

* * *

Of all the crap, crap, crappy nights I've ever had in the whole of my crap life. On a scale of one to 10, we're talking a minus 6. And it's not like I even have very high standards.

* * *

The truth is, some relationships are supposed to last forever, and some are only supposed to last a few days. That's the way life is.

HARRIET TUBMAN

Harriet Tubman (1822 – 1913) was an American abolitionist and political activist. Born into slavery, Tubman escaped and subsequently made some thirteen missions to rescue approximately seventy enslaved people, family, and friends, using the network of antislavery activists and safe houses known as the Underground Railroad.

* * *

Every great dream begins with a dreamer. Always remember, you have within you the strength, the patience, and the passion to reach for the stars to change the world

* * *

I freed a thousand slaves I could have freed a thousand more if only they knew they were slaves.

* * *

I had reasoned this out in my mind, there was one of two things I had a right to, liberty or death; if I could not have one, I would have the other.

* * *

I was the conductor of the Underground Railroad for eight years, and I can say what most conductors can't say; I never ran my train off the track, and I never lost a passenger.

* * *

In my dreams and visions, I seemed to see a line, and on the other side of that line were green fields, and lovely flowers, and beautiful white ladies, who stretched out their arms to me over the line, but I couldn't reach them no-how. I always fell before I got to the line.

* * *

I had crossed the line. I was free, but there was no one to welcome me to the land of freedom. I was a stranger in a strange land.

* * *

I grew up like a neglected weed – ignorant of liberty, having no experience of it.

* * *

I've heard 'Uncle Tom's Cabin' read, and I tell you Mrs. Stowe's pen hasn't begun to paint what slavery is as I have seen it at the far South. I've seen de real thing, and I don't want to see it on no stage or in no theater.

* * *

Never wound a snake; kill it.

* * *

I looked at my hands to see if I was the same person. There was such a glory over everything. The sun came up like gold through the trees, and I felt like I was in heaven.

* * *

I would fight for my liberty so long as my strength lasted, and if the time came for me to go, the Lord would let them take me.

* * *

Quakers are almost as good as colored. They call themselves friends, and you can trust them every time.

* * *

Wasn't me, 'was the Lord! I always told Him, 'I trust to you. I don't know where to go or what to do, but I expect You to lead me,' an' He always did.

* * *

I said to de Lord, 'I'm groin' to hold steady on to you, an' I know you'll see me through.'

* * *

'Pears like I prayed all the time, 'bout my work, everywhere, I prayed an' groaned to the Lord.

* * *

Most of those coming from the mainland are very destitute, almost naked. I am trying to find places for those able to work and provide for them as best I can, so as to lighten the burden on the Government as much as possible, while at the same time they learn to respect themselves by earning their own living.

* * *

As I lay so sick on my bed, from Christmas till March, I was always praying for the poor ole master. 'Pears like I didn't do nothing but pray for the ole master. 'Oh, Lord, convert ole master;' 'Oh, dear Lord, change dat man's heart, and make him a Christian.'

* * *

Lord, I'm going to hold steady on to You, and You've got to see me through.

* * *

I think there's many a slaveholder will get to Heaven. They don't know better. They acts up to the light they have.

* * *

You'll be free or die!

* * *

Read my letter to the old folks, and give my love to them, and tell my brothers to be always watching unto prayer, and when the good old ship of Zion comes along, to be ready to step aboard.

* * *

I can't die but once.

* * *

Pears like my heart go flutter, flutter, and then they may say, 'Peace, Peace,' as much as they likes – I know it's goin' to be war!

* * *

Why, der language down dar in de far South is jus' as different from ours in Maryland, as you can think. Dey laughed when dey heard me talk, an' I could not understand 'dem, no how.

WARREN EDWARD BUFFETT

Warren Edward Buffett (August 30, 1930) - is an American business magnate, investor, philanthropist.

* * *

I never attempt to make money on the stock market. I buy on the assumption that they could close the market the next day and not reopen it for five years.

* * *

Only buy something that you'd be perfectly happy
to hold if the market shut down for 10 years.

* * *

When we own portions of outstanding businesses
with outstanding managements, our favorite
holding period is forever.

* * *

Time is the friend of the wonderful company,
the enemy of the mediocre.

* * *

Opportunities come infrequently.
When it rains gold, put out the bucket,
not the thimble.

* * *

An investor should act as though he had
a lifetime decision card
with just twenty punches on it.

* * *

You only have to do very few things right in your life so long
as you don't do too many things wrong.

* * *

There is nothing wrong with a 'know nothing' investor who realizes it. The problem is when you are a 'know nothing' investor, but you think you know something.

* * *

A horse that can count to ten is a remarkable horse—not a remarkable mathematician.

* * *

It's far better to buy a wonderful company at a fair price than a fair company at a wonderful price.

* * *

Be fearful when others are greedy
and greedy only when others are fearful.

JOHN D. ROCKEFELLER

John Davison Rockefeller (July 8, 1839 – May 23, 1937) - was an American oil industry business magnate and philanthropist.

* * *

Every right implies a responsibility;
every opportunity an obligation,
every possession a duty.

* * *

I believe in the dignity of labor, whether head or hand, that the world owes every person an opportunity to make a living.

* * *

A friendship founded on business is better then a business founded on friendship.

* * *

Charity is injurious unless it helps the recipient to become independent of it.

* * *

Do you know the only thing that gives me pleasure? It's to see my dividends coming in.

* * *

Don't be afraid to give up the good to go for the great.

* * *

Good leadership consists of showing average people how to do the work of superior people.

* * *

The only question with wealth is what you do with it.

* * *

I think it is a man's duty to make all the money he can, keep all that he can and give away all that he can.

* * *

The person who starts simply with the idea of getting rich won't succeed; you must have a larger ambition.

* * *

God gave me money.

I believe the power to make money is a gift from God, to be used and developed to the best of our ability for the best of mankind.

* * *

There's no mystery in business success.
If you do each day's task successfully
and stay faithfully within
these natural operations of commercial laws
which I talk so much about
and keep your head clear,
you will come out all right.

STEVE JOBS

Steve Jobs (February 24, 1955 – October 5, 2011) - was an American entrepreneur, businessman, inventor, and a co-founder of Apple Inc., a member of The Walt Disney Company's board of directors following its acquisition of Pixar.

* * *

We don't get a chance to do that many things,
and everyone should be really excellent.
Because this is our life.
Life is brief, and then you die, you know?
And we've all chosen to do this with our lives.
So, it better be damn good.
It better be worth it.

* * *

That's been one of my mantras — focus and simplicity.
Simple can be harder than complex;
you have to work hard to get your thinking clean
to make it simple.

* * *

Your time is limited,
don't waste it living someone else's life.
Don't be trapped by dogma,
which is living the result of another people's thinking. Don't
let the noise of other opinions
drown your own inner voice.
And most important, have the courage to follow your heart
and intuition, they somehow already know
what you truly want to become.
Everything else is secondary.

* * *

Quality is much better than quantity.
One home run is much better than two doubles.

* * *

Innovation distinguishes between a leader
and a follower.

* * *

Sometimes when you innovate, you make mistakes.
It is best to admit them quickly, and get on with improving
your other innovations.

* * *

I think if you do something and it turns out pretty good, then you should go do something else wonderful, not dwell on it for too long. Just figure out what's next.

* * *

When you're a carpenter making a beautiful chest of drawers, you're not going to use a piece of plywood on the back, even though it faces the wall and nobody will see it. You'll know it's there, so you're going to use a beautiful piece of wood on the back. For you to sleep well at night, the aesthetic, the quality, has to be carried all the way through.

* * *

The design is not just what it looks like and feels like. The design is how it works.

* * *

Creativity is just connecting things. When you ask creative people how they did something, they feel a little guilty because they didn't really do it, they just saw something. It seemed obvious to them after a while.

* * *

My model for business is The Beatles.
They were four guys who kept each other's
kind of negative tendencies in check.
They balanced each other, and the total was greater than the
sum of the parts. That's how I see business:
great things in business are never done by one person,
they're done by a team of people.

* * *

What a computer is to me is the most remarkable tool
that we have ever come up with.
It's the equivalent of a bicycle for our minds.

* * *

Stay hungry.
Stay foolish.

* * *

Here's to the crazy ones, the misfits, the rebels, the
troublemakers, the round pegs in the square holes. The ones
who see things differently are not fond of rules. You can
quote them, disagree with them,
glorify or vilify them, but the only thing you can't-do
is ignore them because they change things.
They push the human race forward,
and while some may see them as the crazy ones,

we see genius, because the ones who are crazy enough to
think that they can change the world,
are the ones who do.

* * *

It's better to be a pirate than to join the navy.

* * *

Be a yardstick of quality.
Some people aren't used to an environment
where excellence is expected.

* * *

You can't connect the dots looking forward;
you can only connect them looking backward.
So you have to trust that the dots
will somehow connect in your future.
You have to trust in something —
your gut, destiny, life, karma, whatever.
This approach has never let me down,
and it has made all the difference in my life.

* * *

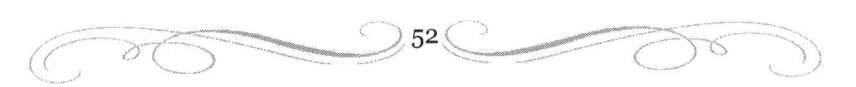

BILL GATES

Bill Gates (born October 28, 1955)
- is a co-founder of the Microsoft Corporation and is an American business magnate, investor, author, and philanthropist.

* * *

Patience is a key element of success.

* * *

It's fine to celebrate success,
but it is more important to heed the lessons of failure.

* * *

People always fear change. People feared electricity when it was invented, didn't they?

* * *

I have been struck again and again by how important measurement is to improving the human condition.

* * *

We always overestimate the change that will occur in the next two years and underestimate the change that will occur in the next ten. Don't let yourself be lulled into inaction.

* * *

Of my mental cycles, I devote maybe 10% to business thinking. Business isn't that complicated. I wouldn't want that on my business card.

* * *

I choose a lazy person to do a hard job. Because a lazy person will find an easy way to do it.

* * *

Don't compare yourself with anyone in this world. If you do so, you are insulting yourself.

KATHERINE MANSFIELD

Kathleen Mansfield Murry (October 14, 1888 –January 9, 1923) was a prominent New Zealand modernist short story writer who was born and brought up in colonial New Zealand and wrote under the pen name of Katherine Mansfield.

* * *

We can do whatever we wish to do provided our wish is strong enough. What do you want most to do? That's what I have to keep asking myself, in the face of difficulties.

* * *

Risk! Risk anything! Care no more for the opinions of others, for those voices. Do the hardest thing on earth for you. Act for yourself. Face the truth.

* * *

I have made it a rule of my life never to regret and never to look back. Regret is an appalling waste of energy… you can't build on it; it's only good for wallowing in.

* * *

When we begin to take our failures non-seriously, it means we are ceasing to be afraid of them.

* * *

I adore life. What do all the fools matter and all the stupidity? They do matter, but somehow for me they cannot touch the body of life. Life is marvelous. I want to be deeply rooted in it – to live – to expand – to breathe in it – to rejoice – to share it. To give and to be asked for love.

* * *

I want, by understanding myself, to understand others. I want to be all that I am capable of becoming.

* * *

The pleasure of all reading is doubled when one lives with another who shares the same books.

* * *

I am going to enjoy life in Paris I know. It is so human, and there is something noble in the city. It is a real city, old and fine and life plays in it for everybody to see.

* * *

I always felt that the great high privilege, relief, and comfort of friendship, was that one had to explain nothing.

* * *

I am treating you as my friend, asking you to share my present minuses in the hope that I can ask you to share my future pluses.

* * *

Could we change our attitude, we should not only see life differently, but life itself would come to be different. Life would undergo a change of appearance because we ourselves had undergone a change of attitude.

* * *

To acknowledge the presence of fear is to give birth to failure.

* * *

I'm a writer first and a woman after.

* * *

Life never becomes a habit to me. It's always a marvel.

* * *

The mind I love must still have wild places, a tangled orchard where dark damsons drop in the heavy grass, an overgrown little wood, the chance of a snake or two, a pool that nobody's fathomed the depth of – and paths threaded with those little flowers planted by the mind.

* * *

I imagine I was always writing. Twaddle it was, too. But better far write twaddle or anything, anything, than nothing at all.

* * *

Were we positive, eager, real – alive? No, we were not. We were a nothingness shot with gleams of what might be.

* * *

If only one could tell true love from false love as one can tell mushrooms from toadstools!

* * *

Everything in life that we really accept undergoes a change. So, suffering must become love. That is the mystery.

* * *

Would you not like to try all sorts of lives – one is so very small – but that is the satisfaction of writing – one can impersonate so many people.

* * *

Care no more for the opinions of others, for those voices. Do the hardest thing on earth for you. Act for yourself. Face the truth.

* * *

I have such a horror of telegrams that ask me how I am! I always want to reply dead.

* * *

It's a terrible thing to be alone – yes, it is, it is – but don't lower your mask until you have another mask prepared beneath – as terrible as you like – but a mask.

* * *

The truth is that every true admirer of the novels cherishes the happy thought that he alone – reading between the lines – has become the secret friend of their author.

* * *

To work – to work! It is such infinite delight to know that we still have the best things to do.

ELON MUSK

Elon Musk (born June 28, 1971) - is a South African-born Canadian American business magnate, investor, engineer, and inventor. Musk is the product architect of Tesla Inc.

* * *

If you get up in the morning and think the future is going to be better, it is a bright day.
Otherwise, it's not.

* * *

If you're trying to create a company, it's like baking a cake. You have to have all the ingredients in the right proportion.

* * *

Patience is a virtue, and I'm learning patience. It's a tough lesson.

* * *

I think it's very important to have a feedback loop, where you're constantly thinking about what you've done and how you could be doing it better.

I think that's the single best piece of advice: constantly think about how you could be doing things better and questioning yourself.

* * *

Life is too short for long-term grudges.

* * *

Some people don't like change, but you need to embrace change if the alternative is disaster.

* * *

I think that's the single best piece of advice: constantly think about how you could be doing things better and questioning yourself.

* * *

The problem is that at a lot of big companies, the process becomes a substitute for thinking. You're encouraged to behave like a little gear in a complex machine. Frankly, it allows you to keep people who aren't that smart, who aren't that creative.

* * *

I do think there is a lot of potential
if you have a compelling product
and people are willing to pay a premium for that.
I think that is what Apple has shown.
You can buy a much cheaper cell phone or laptop,
but Apple's product is so much better
then the alternative,
and people are willing to pay that premium.

* * *

Really, the only thing that makes sense
is to strive for greater collective enlightenment.

* * *

When something is important enough,
you do it even if the odds are not in your favor.

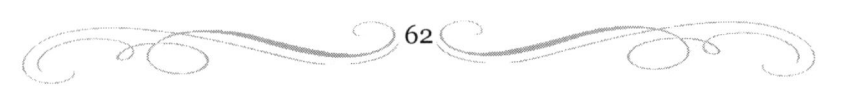

ELIZABETH TAYLOR

Elizabeth Taylor (February 27, 1932—March 23, 2011) One of the film's most celebrated stars, Elizabeth Taylor has fashioned a career that's covered more than six decades, accepting roles that have not only showcased her beauty, but her ability to take on emotionally charged characters

* * *

You find out who your real friends are when you're involved in a scandal.

* * *

My mother says I didn't open my eyes for eight days after I was born, but when I did, the

* * *

first thing I saw was an engagement ring. I was hooked.

* * *

The problem with people who have no vices is that generally, you can be pretty sure they're going to have some pretty annoying virtues.

* * *

Big girls need big diamonds.

* * *

I've only slept with the men I've been married to. How many women can make that claim?

* * *

I've always admitted that I'm ruled by my passions.

* * *

I suppose when they reach a certain age some men are afraid to grow up. It seems the older the men get, the younger their new wives get.

* * *

I, along with the critics, have never taken myself very seriously.

* * *

If someone was stupid enough to offer me a million dollars to make a picture, I'm certainly not dumb enough to turn it down.

* * *

That's the trouble with life – crap dialogue and bad lighting.

* * *

Some of my best leading men have been dogs and horses.

* * *

I feel very adventurous. There are so many doors to be opened, and I'm not afraid to look behind them.

* * *

If not to make the world better, what is money for?

* * *

What is a genius? What is a living legend? What is a megastar? Michael Jackson – that's all. And when you think you know him, he gives you more... I think he is one of the finest people to hit this planet, and, in my estimation, he is the true King of Pop, Rock, and Soul.– Elizabeth Taylor, on Michael Jackson

* * *

I don't think President Bush is doing anything at all about Aids. In fact, I'm not sure he even knows how to spell Aids.

* * *

He is one of the most normal people I know. – Elizabeth Taylor, on Michael Jackson

* * *

Pour yourself a drink, put on some lipstick, and pull yourself together.

* * *

You just do it. You force yourself to get up. You push yourself to put one foot before the other, and God damn it, you refuse to let it get to you. You fight. You cry. You curse. Then you go about the business of living. That's how I've done it. There's no other way.

* * *

I don't pretend to be an ordinary housewife.

* * *

There's still so much more to do. I can't sit back and be complacent, and none of us should be. I get around now in a wheelchair, but I get around.

* * *

Success is a great deodorant. It takes away all your past smells.

I am a very committed wife. And I should be committed too – for being married so many times.

* * *

I've been married too many times. How terrible to change children's affiliations, their affections – to give them the insecurity of placing their trust in someone when maybe that someone won't be there next year.

* * *

I've been through it all, baby, I'm mother courage.

* * *

I don't entirely approve of some of the things I have done, or am, or have been. But I'm me.

* * *

God knows, I'm me.

* * *

The most gorgeous thing in the world and easily one of the best actors.

* * *

The ups and downs, the problems and stress, along with all the happiness, have given me optimism and hope because I am living proof of survival.

* * *

I think I'm finally growing up – and about time. – Elizabeth Taylor, on turning 53 years old

* * *

He is as tough as an old nut and as soft as a yellow ribbon. – Elizabeth Taylor, on John Wayne

* * *

When people say: She's got everything. I've only one answer: I haven't had tomorrow.

* * *

When you're fat, the world is divided into two groups – people who bug you and people who leave you alone. The funny thing is, supporters and saboteurs exist in either camp.

* * *

It's not the having, it's the getting.

* * *

I had a hollow leg. I could drink everyone under the table and not get drunk. My capacity was terrifying.

* * *

I fell off my pink cloud with a thud.

* * *

I have the emotions of a child in the body of a woman. I was rushed into womanhood for the movies. It caused me long moments of unhappiness and doubt.

* * *

I sweat real sweat, and I shake real shakes.

* * *

I really don't remember much about Cleopatra. There were a lot of other things going on.

* * *

I adore wearing gems, but not because they are mine. You can't possess radiance, you can only admire it.

JIM ROHN

Jim Rohn (September 17, 1930 – December 5, 2009) was an American entrepreneur, author, and motivational speaker.

* * *

Don't join an easy crowd; you won't grow.
Go where the expectations and the demands
to perform are high.

* * *

Learn how to be happy with what you have
while you pursue all that you want.

* * *

If you want to be a leader who attracts quality people, the key
is to become a person of quality yourself.

* * *

Profits are better than wages.
Wages make you a living; profits make you a fortune.

* * *

You cannot make progress
without making decisions.

* * *

Formal education will make you a living;
self-education will make you a fortune.

* * *

Motivation alone is not enough.
If you have an idiot and you motivate him,
now you have a motivated idiot.

* * *

One of the greatest gifts you can give to anyone
is the gift of your attention.

* * *

Days are expensive.
When you spend a day
you have one less day to spend.
So, make sure you spend each one wisely.

* * *

Discipline is the bridge
between goals and accomplishment.

* * *

The challenge of leadership
is to be strong, but not rude;
be kind, but not weak;
be bold, but not bully;
be thoughtful, but not lazy;
be humble, but not timid;
be proud, but not arrogant;
have humor but without folly.

* * *

If you really want to do something, you'll find a way.
If you don't, you'll find an excuse.

DALE CARNEGIE

Dale Harbison Carnegie (November 24, 1888 – November 1, 1955) - was an American writer and lecturer and the developer of famous courses in self-improvement, salesmanship, corporate training, public speaking, and interpersonal skills.

* * *

It isn't what you have or who you are or where you are or what you are doing that makes you happy or unhappy. It is what you think about it.

* * *

Talk to someone about themselves
and they'll listen for hours.

* * *

When dealing with people, remember you are not dealing with creatures of logic,
but with creatures bristling with prejudice and motivated by pride and vanity.

* * *

Action seems to follow feeling,
but really action and feeling go together;
and by regulating the action, which is under the more direct
control of the will, we can indirectly regulate the feeling,
which is not.

* * *

The difference between appreciation and flattery? That is
simple. One is sincere and the other insincere.
One comes from the heart out;
the other from the teeth out.
One is unselfish; the other selfish.
One is universally admired;
the other universally condemned.

* * *

I have come to the conclusion
that there is only one way under high heaven
to get the best of an argument – and that is to avoid it.
Avoid it as you would avoid
rattlesnakes and earthquakes.

* * *

Arouse in the other person an eager want.
He who can do this has the whole world with him.
He who cannot walks a lonely way.

Don't be afraid of enemies who attack you.
Be afraid of the friends who flatter you.

* * *

Only knowledge that is used sticks in your mind.

* * *

You can make more friends in two months
by becoming interested in other people
then you can in two years by trying to get other people
interested in you.

* * *

Big shots are only little shots who kept on shooting.

* * *

Winning friends begins with friendliness.

* * *

Criticism is dangerous, because it wounds a person's
precious pride, hurt his sense of importance
and arouses resentment.

BODO SCHAFER

Bodo Schafer (born September 10, 1960) – successful German financial consulter, writer, and businessman.

* * *

It is much better to dare great things,
to celebrate great triumphs,
even when you have had failures along the way,
then to get into the line of the cold and timid souls who
experience neither joy nor pain
because they live in the gray zone
in which there is neither victory nor defeat.

* * *

There is an enormous difference between
playing in order not to lose and playing to win.

* * *

Those who do, expect success.
The one who tries expects that something
will happen.

* * *

Don't think about turning your smartphone off once in a while...think about turning it on once in a while.

* * *

Luck is a result of a lot of work
and careful preparation.

* * *

You will never know what you are capable of
if you are afraid.

THOMAS EDISON

Thomas Alva Edison (February 11, 1847 – October 18, 1931) was an American inventor and businessman.
He developed many devices that greatly influenced life around the world (the phonograph, the motion picture camera, and the long-lasting, practical electric light bulb).

* * *

Our greatest weakness lies in giving up.
The most certain way to succeed
is always to try just one more time.

* * *

Being busy does not always mean real work.
The object of all work is production or accomplishment, and to either of these ends, there must be forethought, system, planning, intelligence, and honest purpose, as well as perspiration.
Seeming to do is not doing.

* * *

Never stop learning.
Read the entire panorama of literature.

* * *

Just because something doesn't do what you planned it to do doesn't mean it's useless.

* * *

There is no substitute for hard work.

* * *

What you are will show in what you do.

* * *

Nearly every man who develops an idea
works it up to the point where it looks impossible, and then
he gets discouraged.
That's not the place to become discouraged.

* * *

The three great essentials to achieving anything worthwhile
are Hard work, Stick-to-itiveness,
and Common sense.

* * *

Maturity is often more absurd than youth
and very frequently is most unjust to youth.

* * *

I never did a day's work in my life. It was all fun.

* * *

Everything comes to him who hustles while he waits.

* * *

I never did anything by accident, nor did any of my
inventions come by accident; they came by work.

ALBERT EINSTEIN

Albert Einstein (14 March 1879 – 18 April 1955)
- was a German-born theoretical physicist.
Einstein developed the theory of relativity,
one of the two pillars of modern physics
(alongside quantum mechanics).

* * *

Few are those who see with their own eyes
and feel with their own hearts.

* * *

Imagination is more important than knowledge. Knowledge
is limited. Imagination encircles the world.

* * *

Unthinking respect for authority
is the greatest enemy of truth.

* * *

Try not to become a man of success, but rather try to become
a man of value.

* * *

Great spirits have always encountered violent opposition
from mediocre minds.

* * *

Not everything that can be counted counts,
and not everything that counts can be counted.

* * *

Everybody is a genius.
But if you judge a fish by its ability to climb a tree,
it will live its whole life believing that it is stupid.

* * *

Look deep into nature,
and then you will understand everything better.

* * *

All religions, arts, and sciences are
branches of the same tree.

* * *

A man should look for what is,
and not for what he thinks should be.

* * *

In the middle of difficulty lies opportunity.

* * *

A person who never made a mistake
never tried anything new.

* * *

Education is what remains after one has forgotten what one has learned in school.

* * *

A human being is part of a whole
called by us the universe.

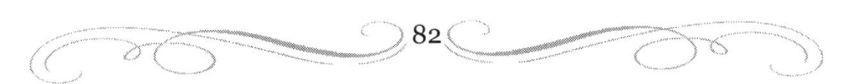

PRINCESS DIANA

Diana, Princess of Wales (July 1, 1961 – August 31, 1997) was a member of the British royal family. She was the first wife of Charles, Prince of Wales, the heir apparent to the British throne, and the mother of Prince William, Duke of Cambridge, and Prince Harry, Duke of Sussex.

* * *

I wear my heart on my sleeve.

* * *

Everyone needs to be valued. Everyone has the potential to give something back.

* * *

Carry out a random act of kindness, with no expectation of reward, safe in the knowledge that one day someone might do the same for you.

* * *

Family is the most important thing in the world.

* * *

Only do what your heart tells you.

* * *

Every one of us needs to show how much we care for each other and, in the process, care for ourselves.

* * *

Life is just a journey.

* * *

They say it is better to be poor and happy than rich and miserable, but how about a compromise like moderately rich and just moody?

* * *

Hugs can do great amounts of good – especially for children.

* * *

If you find someone you love in your life, then hang on to that love.

* * *

The greatest problem in the world today is intolerance. Everyone is so intolerant of each other.

* * *

When you are happy, you can forgive a great deal.

* * *

I don't want expensive gifts; I don't want to be bought. I have everything I want. I just want someone to be there for me, to make me feel safe and secure.

* * *

I touch people. I think everyone needs that. Placing a hand on a friend's face means making contact.

* * *

Helping people in need is a good and essential part of my life, a kind of destiny.

I'd like to be a queen in people's hearts

* * *

Anywhere I see suffering, that is where I want to be, doing what I can.

I don't go by the rulebook; I lead from the heart, not the head.

* * *

You can't comfort the afflicted with afflicting the comfortable.

* * *

I think the biggest disease the world suffers from in this day and age is the disease of people feeling unloved. I know that I can give love for a minute, for half an hour, for a day, for a month, but I can give. I am very happy to do that, I want to do that.

ROBERT KIYOSAKI

Robert Toru Kiyosaki (born April 8, 1947) - is an American businessman and the author. The founder of the Rich Dad Company. The creator of the Cashflow board and software games to educate adults and children business and financial concepts.

* * *

In the real world, the smartest people are people who make mistakes and learn. In school, the smartest people don't make mistakes.

* * *

The trouble with school is they give you the answer, then they give you the exam. That's not life.

* * *

It's not what you say out of your mouth that determines your life. It's what you whisper to yours that has the most power!

* * *

It's more important to grow your income then cut your expenses.

It's more important to grow your spirit
that cut your dreams.

* * *

The most successful people in life
are the ones who ask questions.
They're always learning.
They're always growing.
They're always pushing.

* * *

It's easier to stand on the sidelines, criticize,
and say why you shouldn't do something.
The sidelines are crowded.
Get in the game.

* * *

Don't be addicted to money.
Work to learn, don't work for money.
Work for knowledge.

* * *

Complaining about your current position
in life is worthless. Have a spine and do something about it
instead.

The fear of being different prevents most people from seeking new ways to solve their problems.

* * *

Winners are not afraid of losing.
But losers are.
Failure is part of the process of success.
People who avoid failure also avoid success.

* * *

If you want to be rich, you need to develop your vision. You must be standing on the edge of time gazing into the future.

* * *

If you're still doing what mommy and daddy said for you to do (go to school, get a job, and save money), you're losing.

* * *

Often, the more money you make
the more money you spend;
that's why more money doesn't make you rich –
assets make you rich.

* * *

The most life-destroying word of all
is the word tomorrow.

* * *

The size of your success is measured by
the strength of your desire;
the size of your dream;
and how you handle disappointment along the way.

* * *

I'd rather welcome change
then cling to the past.

THOMAS MORE

Sir Thomas More (7 February 1478 – 6 July 1535) - was an English lawyer, social philosopher, author, statesman and noted Renaissance humanist.

* * *

If honor were profitable,
everybody would be honorable.

* * *

See me safe up for in my coming down,
I can shift for myself.

* * *

I die the king's faithful servant, but God's first.

* * *

And it will fall out as in a complication of diseases, that by applying a remedy to one sore,
you will provoke another;
and that which removes the one ill symptom
produces others.

* * *

There are several sorts of religions, not only in different parts
of the island but even in every town; some worshipping the
sun, others the moon
or one of the planets.

* * *

An absolutely new idea
is one of the rarest things known to man.

* * *

The channel is known only to the natives;
so that if any stranger should enter into the bay without one
of their pilots, he would run
the great danger of shipwreck.

* * *

I would uphold the law if for no other reason
but to protect myself.

* * *

For when they see the people swarm into the streets, and
daily wet to the skin with rain,
and yet cannot persuade them to go out of the rain, they do
keep themselves within their houses,
seeing they cannot remedy the folly of the people.

And, indeed, though they differ concerning other things, yet
all agree in this:
that they think there is one Supreme Being
that made and governs the world, whom they call, in the
language of their country, Mithras.

NANCY ASTOR

Nancy Witcher Langhorne Astor (May 19, 1879 – May 2, 1964) was the first female Member of Parliament to take her seat.

* * *

I married beneath me, all women do.

* * *

If I were your wife, I'd put poison in your coffee. If I were your husband, I'd drink it.

* * *

We, women, talk too much, but even then, we don't tell half what we know.

* * *

I used to dread getting older because I thought I would not be able to do all the things I wanted to do, but now that I am older, I find that I don't want to do them.

* * *

One reason I don't drink is that I want to know when I am having a good time.

* * *

A fool without fear is sometimes wiser than an angel with fear.

The trouble with most people is that they think with their hopes or fears or wishes rather than with their minds.

* * *

In passing, also, I would like to say that the first time Adam had a chance, he laid the blame on a woman.

* * *

The most practical thing in the world is common sense and common humanity.

* * *

Pioneers may be picturesque figures, but they are often rather lonely ones.

* * *

The main dangers in this life are the people who want to change everything or nothing.

* * *

Dreams are great. When they disappear, you may still be here, but you will have ceased to live.

* * *

Women have got to make the world safe for men since men have made it so darned unsafe for women.

* * *

Truth always originates in a minority of one, and every custom begins as a broken precedent.

* * *

Take a close-up of a woman past sixty? You might as well use a picture of a relief map of Ireland!

* * *

My vigor, vitality, and cheek repel me – I am the kind of woman I would run from.

The penalty of success is to be bored by people who used to snub you.

* * *

Real education should educate us out of self into something far finer; into a selflessness which links us with all humanity.

* * *

The only thing I like about rich people is their money.

FERDINAND PORSCHE

Ferdinand Porsche (3 September 1875 – 30 January 1951) - was an automotive engineer and founder of the Porsche car company.

* * *

I couldn't find the sports car of my dreams, so I built it myself.

* * *

If one does not fail at times, then one has not challenged himself.

* * *

Design must be functional, and functionality must be translated into visual aesthetics without any reliance on gimmicks that have to be explained.

* * *

I came into the world at the same time as the auto, if you will.

MARGARET THATCHER

Margaret Thatcher (13 October 1925 – 8 April 2013) - was a British stateswoman was Prime Minister of the United Kingdom from 1979 to 1990 and Leader of the Conservative Party from 1975 to 1990.

* * *

What is a success?
I think it is a mixture of having a flair for the thing that you are doing; knowing that it is not enough,
that you have got to have hard work
and a certain sense of purpose.

* * *

I always cheer up immensely if an attack is particularly wounding because I think, well, if they attack one personally, it means they have not a single political argument left.

* * *

I love argument. I love debate.
I don't expect anyone just to sit there and agree with me,
that's not their job.

* * *

Any woman who understands the problems of running a home will be nearer to understanding the problems of running a country.

* * *

Being powerful is like being a lady. If you have to tell people you are, you aren't.

* * *

Disciplining yourself to do what you know is right and important, although difficult, is the high road to pride, self-esteem, and personal satisfaction.

* * *

If you want something said, ask a man; if you want something done, ask a woman.

* * *

I am extraordinarily patient, provided I get my own way in the end.

* * *

To wear your heart on your sleeve isn't a very good plan; you should wear it inside, where it functions best.

* * *

I usually make up my mind about a man
in ten seconds, and I very rarely change it.

* * *

You may have to fight a battle more
than once to win it.

* * *

I've got a woman's ability to stick to a job
and get on with it when everyone else
walks off and leaves it.

* * *

Defeat? I do not recognize the meaning of the word.

* * *

It pays to know the enemy – not least because at some time
you may have the opportunity
to turn him into a friend.

* * *

It is not the creation of wealth that is wrong,
but the love of money for its own sake.

* * *

There is no such thing as society.
There are individual men and women
and there are families.

* * *

I don't mind how much my ministers talk,
as long as they do what I say.

* * *

I am not a consensus politician.
I'm a conviction politician.

WINSTON CHURCHILL

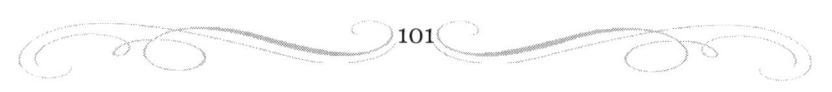

Winston Churchill (30 November 1874 – 24 January 1965) was a British politician and statesman who served as the Prime Minister of the United Kingdom.
As Prime Minister, Churchill led Britain to the victory over Nazi Germany during World War II.

* * *

Attitude is a little thing that makes a BIG difference.

* * *

Success is not final, failure is not fatal,
it is the courage to continue that counts.

* * *

If you're going through hell, keep going.

* * *

History will be kind to me, for I intend to write it.

* * *

A pessimist sees the difficulty in every opportunity,
an optimist sees the opportunity in every difficulty.

When the eagles are silent, the parrots begin to jabber.

* * *

Out of intense complexities,
intense simplicities emerge.

* * *

Courage is what it takes to stand up and speak,
it's also what it takes to sit down and listen.

BRUCE LEE

Bruce Lee (November 27, 1940 – July 20, 1973)
– Chinese American; the creator of Jeet Kune Do;
the film director, screenwriter, martial artist, philosopher,
actor, and producer.

* * *

If you always put limits on everything you do, physical or anything else, it will spread into your work and into your life. There are no limits. There are only plateaus, and you must not stay there, you must go beyond them.

* * *

I fear not the man who has practiced 10 000 kicks once, but I fear the man who has practiced
one kick 10 000 times.

* * *

A goal is not always meant to be reached,
it often serves simply as something to aim at.

* * *

Knowing is not enough; We must apply.
Willing is not enough; We must do.

* * *

Mistakes are always forgivable if one has the courage to admit them.

* * *

Defeat is a state of mind; No one is ever defeated until defeat has been accepted as a reality.

* * *

Those who are unaware they are walking in darkness will never seek the light.

* * *

To hell with circumstances;
I create opportunities.

* * *

Absorb what is useful, discard what is not,
add what is uniquely your own.

* * *

Learning is never cumulative;
it is a movement of knowing which has
no beginning and no end.

* * *

Do not pray for an easy life,
pray for the strength
to endure a difficult one.

SOPHIA LOREN

Sofia Villani Scicolone, known by her stage name Sophia Loren (born September 20, 934) is an Italian film actress and singer.

* * *

Nothing makes a woman more beautiful than the belief that she is beautiful.

* * *

Everything you see I owe to pasta.

* * *

Sex is like washing your face – just something you do because you have to. Sex without love is absolutely ridiculous. Sex follows love, it never precedes it.

* * *

There is a fountain of youth: It is your mind, your talents, the creativity you bring to your life and the lives of people you love. When you learn to tap this source, you will have truly defeated age.

* * *

Many people think they want things, but they don't really have the strength, the discipline. They are weak. I believe that you get what you want if you want it badly enough.

* * *

When you are a mother, you are never really alone in your thoughts. A mother always has to think twice, once for herself and once for her child

* * *

The only people who never make mistakes are the ones who don't do anything. Mistakes are part of the dues one pays for living a full life.

* * *

If you haven't cried, your eyes cannot be beautiful.

* * *

It's a mistake to think that once you're done with school, you need never learn anything new.

* * *

If you can learn to use your mind as well as your powder puff, you will become more truly beautiful.

* * *

I've never tried to block out the memories of the past, even though some are painful. I don't understand people who hide from their past. Everything you live through helps to make you the person you are now.

* * *

Beauty is how you feel inside, and it reflects in your eyes. It is not something physical.

* * *

I hated my father all my life, but in his final days, I forgave him for all the suffering he caused us. As you grow older, marry, and have children of your own, you learn and forget. I do not forget easily, but I do forgive.

* * *

I was not interested in what I could bring to myself by being an actress, but in what I could bring out of myself.

* * *

I'm not Italian, I am Neapolitan! It's another thing.

* * *

True happiness is impossible without solitude.... I need solitude in my life as I need food and drink and the laughter of little children. Extravagant though it may sound, solitude is the filter of my soul. It nourishes me and rejuvenates me. Left alone, I discovered that I keep myself good company.

* * *

When – Sophia Loren is naked, that is a lot of nakedness

* * *

It is very important for an actor or actress to look around at everything and everyone and never forget about real life.

* * *

Being beautiful can never hurt, but you have to have more. You have to sparkle, you have to be fun, you have to make your brain work if you have one.

* * *

The facts of life are that a child who has seen war cannot be compared with a child who doesn't know what war is except from television.

* * *

You give but little when you give of your possessions. It is when you give of yourself that you truly give.

* * *

I think the quality of sexiness comes from within. It is something that is in you, or it isn't, and it really doesn't have much to do with breasts or thighs or the pout of your lips.

* * *

My philosophy is that it's better to explore life and make mistakes than to play it safe and not to explore at all.

* * *

Sex appeal is fifty percent what you've got and fifty percent what people think you've got.

* * *

I do not have a set regimen of exercise. The only activity I really enjoy is swimming. And I love to walk for long distances.

* * *

I firmly believe we can make our own miracles if we believe strongly enough in ourselves and our mission on earth.

* * *

I always wake up early and jump out of bed – sometimes not wanting to, because one can always find an alibi not to exercise – and then I take a walk for an hour. And as I walk around the park I always think, maybe around the corner, I am going to find something beautiful. I always think positively. It is very rare that you find me in a mood that is sad or melancholic.

* * *

The two big advantages I had at birth were to have been born wise and have been born in poverty.

* * *

A woman's dress should be like a barbed-wire fence, serving its purpose without obstructing the view.

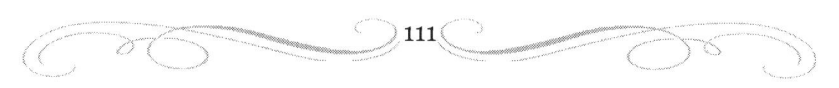

MIKE TYSON

Mike Tyson (born June 30, 1966) - American boxer. His record is at 50 wins, 5 losses, 2 no contests (44 knockout wins).

* * *

When you have something in life that you want to accomplish great, you have to be willing to give up your happiness.
I've lost all my sensitivity as far as being embarrassed, being shy, you just have to lose that.

* * *

I put people in body bags
when I'm right.

* * *

My intentions were not to fascinate the world
with my personality.

* * *

Don't be surprised if I behave like a savage.
I am a savage.

I'm just trying to change my life because I'm not above killing any drug dealer for money.

* * *

A lot of people don't like themselves, and I happen to be totally in love with myself.

* * *

I think the reality of prison is you don't get anything unless you want it in there. Whatever happens to you in prison, this is what you asked for.
Nothing happens to you if you don't give that vibe.

* * *

I've been a prima-donna. I was taken care of since I was 13. That's why I am the way I am today. I was spoiled, like a brat. I had anything I wanted. That's crazy to be that way all your life. Everybody's taking care of you, but manipulating you at the same time. Very few people have a life like that. Most people have to work like slaves their whole lives. I've never had a job in my life. What I know how to do is hurt big, tough men - in the street and off.

MUHAMMAD ALI

Muhammad Ali (January 17, 1942 – June 3, 2016) – was an American boxer and activist.
Ali is regarded as one of the leading heavyweight boxers of the 20th century.

* * *

Float like a butterfly, sting like a bee.

* * *

Don't count the days. Make the days count.

* * *

Impossible is temporary. Impossible is nothing.

* * *

If my mind can conceive it if my heart can believe it-then I can achieve it.

* * *

I am the greatest. I said that even before I knew I was.

* * *

A man who has no imagination has no wings.

* * *

It isn't the mountains ahead to climb that wear you out; it's the pebble in your shoe.

* * *

He who is not courageous enough to take risks will accomplish nothing in life.

JOAN CRAWFORD

Joan Crawford (March 23, 1904 - May 10, 1977) was an American actress who began her career as a dancer and stage showgirl. In 1999, the American Film Institute ranked Crawford tenth on its list of the greatest female stars of Classic Hollywood Cinema.

* * *

Don't fuck with me, fellas. This cowgirl has been to the rodeo before.

* * *

Working with Bette Davis on Whatever Happened to Baby Jane was one of the greatest challenges I ever had. And I mean that kindly. Bette is of a different temperament than I. Bette had to scream and yell every morning. I just sat and knitted. I knitted a scarf from Hollywood to Malibu.

* * *

You have to be self-reliant and strong to survive in this town. Otherwise, you will be destroyed.

* * *

I love playing bitches. There's a lot of bitch in every woman – a lot in every man.

* * *

Love is a fire. But whether it is going to warm your hearth or burn down your house, you can never tell.

* * *

Any actress who appears in public without being well-groomed is digging her own grave.

* * *

Hollywood is like life. You face it with the sum total of your equipment.

* * *

I'd like to think every director I've worked with has fallen in love with me.

* * *

Find your own style and have the courage to stick to it.

* * *

Choose your clothes for your way of life.

* * *

Make your wardrobe as versatile as an actress. It should be able to play many roles.

Find your happiest colors – the ones that make you feel good.

* * *

Care for your clothes, like the good friends they are!

* * *

I have always known what I wanted, and that was beauty... in every form

* * *

I was born in front of a camera and really don't know anything else.

* * *

I never go outside unless I look like – Joan Crawford the movie star. If you want to see the girl next door, go next door.

* * *

If I can't be me, I don't want to be anybody.

* * *

Send me flowers while I'm alive. They won't do me a damn bit of good when I'm dead.

* * *

I think that the most important thing a woman can have – next to talent, of course – is her hairdresser.

* * *

It has been said that on screen I personified the American woman.

* * *

There was a saying around MGM – Norma Shearer got the productions, Greta Garbo supplied the art, and – Joan Crawford made money to pay for both.

* * *

I believe in the dollar. Everything I earn, I spend!

* * *

I need sex for a clear complexion, but I'd rather do it for love.

* * *

If you've earned a position, be proud of it. Don't hide it. I want to be recognized. When I hear people say, There's – Joan Crawford! I turn around and say, Hi! How are you?

* * *

The Democratic party is one that I've always observed. I have struggled greatly in life from the day I was born, and I am honored to be a part of something that focuses on working-class citizens and molds them into a proud specimen. Mr. Roosevelt and Mr. Kennedy have done so much in that regard for the two generations they've won over during their career course.

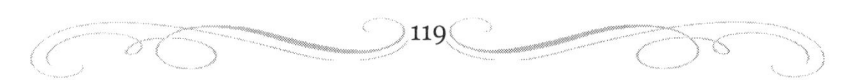

AMELIA EARHART

Amelia Mary Earhart (born July 24, 1897; disappeared July 2, 1937) was an American female aviation pioneer and author.

* * *

Please know that I am aware of the hazards. I want to do it because I want to do it. Women must try to do things as men have tried. When they fail, their failure must be but a challenge to others.

* * *

Courage is the price that life exacts for granting peace. The soul that knows it not, knows no release from little things, knows not the livid loneliness of fear.

* * *

The most difficult thing is the decision to act, the rest is merely tenacity. The fears are paper tigers. You can do anything you decide to do. You can act to change and control your life, and the procedure, the process is its own reward.

* * *

No kind action ever stops with itself. One kind action leads to another. Good example is followed.

* * *

Women must pay for everything. They do get more glory than men for comparable feats, But they also get more notoriety when they crash.

* * *

Women, like men, should try to do the impossible. And when they fail, their failure should be a challenge to others.

* * *

Worry retards reaction and makes clear-cut decisions impossible.

* * *

Everyone has ocean's to fly if they have the heart to do it. Is it reckless?
Maybe – but what do dreams know of boundaries?

* * *

The more one does and sees and feels, the more one is able to do, and the more genuine may be one's appreciation of fundamental things like home, and love, and understanding companionship.

* * *

Never interrupt someone doing something you said couldn't be done.

* * *

Adventure is worthwhile in itself.

* * *

A single act of kindness throws out roots in all directions, and the roots spring up and make new trees. The greatest work that kindness does to others is that it makes them kind themselves.

* * *

Anticipation, I suppose, sometimes exceeds realization.

* * *

In my life, I had come to realize that when things were going very well, indeed it was just the time to anticipate trouble. And, conversely, I learned from pleasant experience that at the most despairing crisis, when all looked sour beyond words, some delightful break was apt to lurk just around the corner.

* * *

I want to do something useful in the world.

* * *

Preparation, I have often said, is rightly two-thirds of any venture.

* * *

Being alone is scary, but not as scary as feeling alone in a relationship.

* * *

Better do a good deed near at home than go far away to burn incense.

* * *

Experiment! Meet new people. That's better than any college education.

* * *

After midnight the moon set and I was alone with the stars. I have often said that the lure of flying is the lure of beauty, and I need no other flight to convince me that the reason flyers fly, whether they know it or not, is the aesthetic appeal of flying.

* * *

Flying may not be all plain sailing, but the fun of it is worth the price.

* * *

The most effective way to do it is to do it.

WILL SMITH

Willard Carroll "Will" Smith Jr. (born September 25, 1968) - is an American actor, producer, rapper, comedian, and songwriter. Smith has won four Grammy Awards.

* * *

Throughout life, people will make you mad,
disrespect you and treat you bad.
Let God deal with the things they do,
cause hate in your heart will consume you too.

* * *

The first step is you have to say that you can.

* * *

There's no reason to have a plan B
because it distracts from plan A.

* * *

I wake up every morning
believing today is going to be better than yesterday.

* * *

Smiling is the best way to face every problem,
to crush every fear and to hide every pain.

* * *

If you don't fight for what you want,
don't cry for what you lost.

* * *

Never underestimate the pain of a person,
because in all honesty, everyone is struggling,
some people are just better at hiding it than others.

* * *

Let your smile change the world.
Don't let the world change your smile.

* * *

Look at your 5 closest friends.
Those 5 friends are who you are.
If you don't like who you are
then you know what you have to do.

* * *

You don't set out to build a wall.
You don't say 'I'm going to build the biggest,
greatest wall that's ever been built.'
You don't start there. You say, 'I'm going to lay this brick as
perfectly as a brick can be laid.'
You do that every single day.
And soon you have a wall.

* * *

Greatness exists
in all of us.

* * *

Sometimes you have to forget what's gone,
appreciate what still remains,
and look forward to what's
coming next.

* * *

Money and success don't change people;
they merely amplify what is already there.

* * *

I'm a student of world religion, so to me,
it's hugely important to have knowledge
and to understand what people are doing.

* * *

I've viewed myself as slightly above average in talent. And
where I excel is ridiculous, sickening work ethic.

* * *

In black neighborhoods, everybody appreciated comedy
about real life. In the white community, fantasy was funnier.
I started looking for the jokes that were equally hilarious
across the board, for totally different reasons.

* * *

I want the world to be better because I was here.

* * *

It's quite highly possible that I have peaked.
I mean, I just can't imagine what else I could do beyond this.
It's really a bittersweet kind of feeling.

* * *

Whatever your dream is,
every extra penny you have needs
to be going to that.

* * *

If it was something that I really committed myself to, I don't
think there's anything that could stop me becoming a
President of the United States.

* * *

When I was growing up,
I installed refrigerators in supermarkets.
My father was an electrical engineer.

JOHN C. MAXWELL

John Calvin Maxwell (born 1947)
- is an American author, speaker, and pastor who has written many books, primarily focusing on leadership.

* * *

Leadership is not about titles, positions or flowcharts. It is about one life influencing another.

* * *

A great leader's courage to fulfill his vision comes from passion, not position.

* * *

A leader is one who knows the way, goes the way and shows the way.

* * *

Leaders must be close enough to relate to others, but far enough ahead to motivate them.

* * *

A leader who produces other leaders
multiplies their influences.

* * *

Real leadership is being the person
others will gladly and confidently follow.

* * *

If you wouldn't follow yourself,
why should anyone else?

* * *

When the leader lacks confidence,
the followers lack commitment.

* * *

The higher you want to climb,
the more you need leadership.
The greater the impact you want to make,
the greater your influence needs to be.

* * *

If you can't influence people,
then they will not follow you.

And if people won't follow, you are not a leader.
That's the Law of Influence.

* * *

Anyone can steer the ship, but it takes
a leader to chart the course.
Leaders who are good navigators
are capable of taking their people just about anywhere.

* * *

If you want to be a leader,
the good news is that you can do it.
Everyone has the potential,
but it isn't accomplished overnight.
It requires perseverance.

* * *

Managers work with processes-
leaders work with people.

* * *

Everything rises and falls on leadership.

* * *

Good leaders know when to display emotions
and when to delay them.

* * *

Do you know the difference between
leaders, followers, and losers?
Leaders stretch with challenges.
Followers struggle with challenges.
Losers shrink from challenges.

* * *

To lead any way other than by example,
we send a fuzzy picture of leadership to others.
If we work on improving ourselves first
and make that our primary mission,
then others are more likely to follow.

* * *

All true leaders have learned to say no to the good
in order to say yes to the best.

* * *

The best leaders are humble enough
to realize their victories, depend
upon their people.

* * *

Leaders see everything with a leadership bias.
Their focus is on mobilizing people
and leveraging resources to achieve their goals
rather than on using their own individual efforts. Leaders who want to succeed
maximize every asset and resource they have
for the benefit of their organization.
For that reason, they are continually aware of
what they have at their disposal.

* * *

It's not the position that makes the leader;
it's the leader that makes the position.

NAPOLEON BONAPARTE

Napoleon Bonaparte (15 August 1769 – 5 May 1821) - was a French military and political leader. He was the Emperor of the French.

* * *

If you want a thing done well, do it yourself.

* * *

A leader is a dealer in hope.

* * *

Never interrupt your enemy when he is making a mistake.

* * *

Impossible is a word to be found only in the dictionary of fools.

* * *

Great ambition is the passion of a great character. Those endowed with it may perform very good or very bad acts. All depends on the principles which direct them.

Victory belongs to the most persevering.

* * *

Glory is fleeting, but obscurity is forever.

* * *

Ability is nothing without opportunity.

* * *

A true man hates no one.

* * *

I made all my generals out of the mud.

CONFUCIUS

Confucius (September 28, 551 BC – 479 BC) - was a Chinese teacher, editor, politician, and philosopher of the Spring and Autumn period of Chinese history.

* * *

Everything has its beauty, but not everyone sees it.

* * *

Never impose on others what you would not choose for yourself.

* * *

It does not matter how slowly you go so long as you do not stop.

* * *

He, who learns but does not think, is lost. He who thinks but does not learn is in great danger.

* * *

Choose a job you love and you will never have to work a day in your life.

* * *

If a man takes no thought about what is distant, he will find sorrow near at hand.

* * *

The cautious seldom err.

* * *

To know what you know and
what you do not know,
that is true knowledge.

* * *

The superior man is modest in his speech
but exceeds in his actions.

* * *

He who wishes to secure the good of others
has already secured his own.

* * *

To see the right and not
to do it is cowardice.

* * *

Wisdom, compassion, and courage
are the three universally recognized
moral qualities of men.

* * *

Better a diamond with a flaw
then a pebble without.

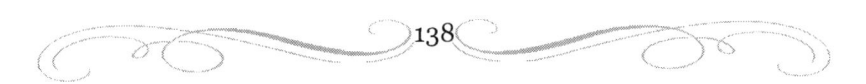

SUN TZU

Sun Tzu (544 BC – 496 BC)
- was a Chinese general, military strategist, and philosopher. Sun Tzu is traditionally credited as the author of "The Art of War."

* * *

The supreme art of war is
to subdue the enemy without fighting.

* * *

Invincibility lies in the defense;
the possibility of victory in the attack.

* * *

He will win who knows when to fight and when not to fight.

* * *

If you know the enemy and know yourself you need not fear the results of a hundred battles.

* * *

Victorious warriors win first and then go to war, while defeated warriors go to war first and then seek to win.

* * *

Pretend inferiority and encourage his arrogance.

* * *

Victory usually goes to the army who has better trained officers and men.

* * *

If your opponent is of choleric temper, irritate him.

* * *

He who knows when he can fight and when he cannot will be victorious.

* * *

All men can see these tactics whereby I conquer, but what none can see is the strategy out of which victory is evolved.

* * *

Prohibit the taking of omens, and do away with superstitious doubts. Then, until death itself comes, no calamity need be feared.

GENGHIS KHAN

Genghis Khan (c. 1162 – August 18, 1227) - was the Great Khan and founder of the Mongol Empire, which became the largest contiguous empire in the history after his death.

* * *

Violence never settles anything.

* * *

One arrow alone can be easily broken
but many arrows are indestructible.

* * *

Be of one mind and one faith,
that you may conquer your enemies
and lead long and happy lives.

* * *

The pleasure and joy of man
lies in treading down the rebel
and conquering the enemy,
in tearing him up by the root,
in taking from him all that he has.

* * *

There is no good in anything
until it is finished.

* * *

Even when a friend does something
you do not like, he continues
to be your friend.

* * *

It is not sufficient that
I succeed - all others must fail.

* * *

Those who were adept and brave fellows
I have made military commanders.
Those who were quick and nimble
I have made herders of horses.
Those who were not adept
I have given a small whip and sent
to be shepherds.

* * *

Remember, you have no companions but your shadow.

GAIUS JULIUS CAESAR

Gaius Julius Caesar (20 BC – 21 February 4 AD) - was the adopted son and heir of Augustus. Roman politician, commander, writer.

* * *

In the end, it is impossible not to become what others believe you are.

* * *

Experience is the teacher of all things.

* * *

The greatest enemy will hide in the last place, you would ever look.

* * *

No one is so brave that he is not disturbed by something unexpected.

* * *

I love the name of honor more
than I fear death.

* * *

Men are nearly always willing to believe
what they wish.

* * *

Without training, they lacked knowledge.
Without knowledge, they lacked confidence.
Without confidence, they lacked victory.

* * *

It is better to create than to learn!
Creating is the essence of life.

* * *

If you must break the law, do it to seize power:
in all other cases observe it.

* * *

I love treason but hate a traitor.

* * *

All bad precedents begin as justifiable measures.

* * *

Divide and Conquer.

* * *

It is easier to find men who will volunteer to die
then to find those who are willing to
endure pain with patience.

* * *

I came to Rome when it was a city of stone
and left it a city of marble.

ANNA ELEANOR ROOSEVELT

Anna Eleanor Roosevelt (October 11, 1884 – November 7, 1962) was an American political figure, diplomat and activist. She served as the First Lady of the United States from March 1933 to April 1945.

* * *

Do what you feel in your heart to be right – for you'll be criticized anyway. You'll be damned if you do, and damned if you don't.

* * *

The future belongs to those who believe in the beauty of their dreams.

* * *

The purpose of life is to live it, to taste experience to the utmost, to reach out eagerly and without fear for newer and richer experience.

* * *

Do one thing every day that scares you.

* * *

You must do the things you think you cannot do.

* * *

A stumbling block to the pessimist is a stepping-stone to the optimist.

* * *

It is better to light a candle than curse the darkness.

* * *

You can often change your circumstances by changing your attitude.

* * *

Many people will walk in and out of your life, but only true friends will leave footprints in your heart.

* * *

Do one thing every day that scares you.

* * *

In the long run, we shape our lives, and we shape ourselves. The process never ends until we die. And the choices we make are ultimately our own responsibility.

* * *

Justice cannot be for one side alone but must be for both.

* * *

It takes courage to love, but pain through love is the purifying fire which those who love generously know.

* * *

If life were predictable, it would cease to be life, and be without flavor.

* * *

We are afraid to care too much, for fear that the other person does not care at all.

* * *

The only things one can admire at length are those one admires without knowing why.

* * *

The giving of love is an education in itself.

* * *

The battle for the individual rights of women is one of long standing, and none of us should countenance anything which undermines it.

* * *

Perhaps nature is our best assurance of immortality.

* * *

Sometimes I wonder if we shall ever grow up in our politics and say definite things which mean something, or whether we shall always go on using generalities to which everyone can subscribe, and which mean very little.

* * *

Happiness is not a goal... it's a by-product of a life well lived.

* * *

You gain strength, courage, and confidence by every experience in which you really stop to look fear in the face. You are able to say to yourself, 'I have lived through this horror. I can take the next thing that comes along.' You must do the thing you think you cannot do.

* * *

A woman is like a tea bag – you can't tell how strong she is until you put her in hot water.

* * *

Too often the great decisions are originated and given form in bodies made up wholly of men, or so completely dominated by them that whatever of special value women have to offer is shunted aside without expression.

* * *

Only a man's character is the real criterion of worth.

* * *

To handle yourself, use your head; to handle others, use your heart.

* * *

You wouldn't worry so much about what others think of you if you realized how seldom they do.

* * *

My experience has been that work is almost the best way to pull oneself out of the depths.

* * *

It isn't enough to talk about peace. One must believe in it. And it isn't enough to believe in it. One must work at it.

* * *

I think, at a child's birth if a mother could ask a fairy godmother to endow it with the most useful gift, that gift should be curiosity.

* * *

When will our consciences grow so tender that we will act to prevent human misery rather than avenge it?

* * *

Have convictions. Be friendly. Stick to your beliefs as they stick to theirs. Work as hard as they do.

* * *

Every time you meet a situation you think at the time it is an impossibility, and you go through the tortures of the damned, once you have met it and lived through it, you find that forever after you are freer than you were before.

* * *

I think that somehow, we learn who we really are and then live with that decision.

* * *

Beautiful young people are accidents of nature, but beautiful old people are works of art.

* * *

I once had a rose named after me, and I was very flattered. But I was not pleased to read the description in the catalog: no good in a bed, but fine up against a wall.

* * *

No one can make you feel inferior without your consent.

* * *

Do the things that interest you and do them with all your heart. Don't be concerned about whether people are watching you or criticizing you.

* * *

A little simplification would be the first step toward rational living, I think.

* * *

What you don't do can be a destructive force.

* * *

People grow through experience if they meet life honestly and courageously. This is how the character is built.

* * *

You gain strength, courage, and confidence by every experience in which you really stop to look fear in the face. You are able to say to yourself, 'I lived through this horror. I can take the next thing that comes along.

* * *

What one has to do usually can be done.

* * *

I think I lived those years very impersonally. It was almost as though I had erected someone outside myself who was the president's wife. I was lost somewhere deep down inside myself. That is the way I felt and worked until I left the White House.

* * *

It is not fair to ask of others what you are not willing to do yourself.

* * *

Probably the happiest period in life most frequently is in middle age, when the eager passions of youth are cooled, and the infirmities of age not yet begun; as we see that the shadows, which are at morning and evening so large, almost entirely disappear at midday.

* * *

You can't move so fast that you try to change the mores faster than people can accept it. That doesn't mean you do nothing, but it means that you do the things that need to be done according to priority.

* * *

Courage is exhilarating.

* * *

With the new day comes new strength and new thoughts.

* * *

I'm so glad I never feel important, it does complicate life!

* * *

In all our contacts it is probably the sense of being really needed and wanted which gives us the greatest satisfaction and creates the most lasting bond.

* * *

If someone betrays you once, it's their fault; if they betray you twice, it's your fault.

* * *

We do not have to become heroes overnight. Just a step at a time, meeting each thing that comes up, seeing it as not as dreadful as it appears, discovering that we have the strength to stare it down.

* * *

What could we accomplish if we knew we could not fail?

* * *

Probably the happiest period in life most frequently is in middle age, when the eager passions of youth are cooled, and the infirmities of age not yet begun; as we see that the shadows, which are at morning and evening so large, almost entirely disappear at midday.

* * *

You can never really live anyone else's life, not even your child's. The influence you exert is through your own life, and what you've become yourself.

* * *

Autobiographies are only useful as the lives you read about and analyze may suggest to you something that you may find useful in your own journey through life.

* * *

In the long run, we shape our lives, and we shape ourselves. The process never ends until we die. And the choices we make are ultimately our own responsibility.

* * *

Pit race against race, religion against religion, prejudice against prejudice. Divide and conquer! We must not let that happen here.

* * *

I can not believe that war is the best solution. No one won the last war, and no one will win the next war.

* * *

I do not think that I am a natural born mother… If I ever wanted to mother anyone, it was my father.

* * *

Old age has deformities enough of its own. It should never add to them the deformity of vice.

* * *

One's philosophy is not best expressed in words; it is expressed in the choices one makes… and the choices we make are ultimately our responsibility.

* * *

Never allow a person to tell you know who doesn't have the power to say yes.

✳ ✳ ✳

As for accomplishments, I just did what I had to do as things came along.

✳ ✳ ✳

I have never felt that anything really mattered but knowing that you stood for the things in which you believed and had done the very best you could.

✳ ✳ ✳

You have to accept whatever comes and the only important thing is that you meet it with courage and with the best that you have to give.

✳ ✳ ✳

A mature person is one who does not think only in absolutes, who is able to be objective even when deeply stirred emotionally, who has learned that there is both good and bad in all people and in all things, and who walks humbly and deals charitably with the circumstances of life, knowing that in this world no one is all-knowing, and therefore all of us need both love and charity.

✳ ✳ ✳

Great minds discuss ideas; average minds discuss events; small minds discuss people.

✳ ✳ ✳

The only advantage of not being too good a housekeeper is that your guests are so pleased to feel how very much better they are.

* * *

The reason that fiction is more interesting than any other form of literature, to those who really like to study people, is that in fiction the author can really tell the truth without humiliating himself.

* * *

Happiness is not a goal; it is a by-product.

* * *

Never mistake knowledge for wisdom. One helps you make a living; the other helps you make a life.

* * *

Ambition is pitiless. Any merit that it cannot use it finds despicable.

* * *

Since you get more joy out of giving joy to others, you should put a good deal of thought into the happiness that you are able to give.

* * *

Today is the oldest you've ever been, and the youngest you'll ever be again.

* * *

I used to tell my husband that, if he could make me 'understand' something, it would be clear to all the other people in the country.

* * *

Hate and force cannot be in just a part of the world without having an effect on the rest of it.

* * *

Understanding is a two-way street.

* * *

Freedom makes a huge requirement of every human being. With freedom comes responsibility. For the person who is unwilling to grow up, the person who does not want to carry his own weight, this is a frightening prospect.

* * *

One thing life has taught me: if you are interested, you never have to look for new interests. They come to you. When you are genuinely interested in one thing, it will always lead to something else.

* * *

Do not stop thinking of life as an adventure. You have no security unless you can live bravely, excitingly, imaginatively; unless you can choose a challenge instead of competence.

* * *

I have spent many years of my life in opposition, and I rather like the role.

* * *

Anyone who thinks must think of the next war as they would of suicide.

* * *

The mother of a family should look upon her housekeeping and the planning of meals as a scientific occupation.

* * *

I believe that anyone can conquer fear by doing the things he fears to do, provided he keeps doing them until he gets a record of successful experience behind him.

* * *

Life was meant to be lived, and curiosity must be kept alive. One must never, for whatever reason, turn his back on life.

* * *

When life is too easy for us, we must beware, or we may not be ready to meet the blows which sooner or later come to everyone, rich or poor.

* * *

Remember always that you have not only the right to be an individual; you have an obligation to be one. You cannot make any useful contribution in life unless you do this.

* * *

Never be bored, and you will never be boring.

* * *

I am who I am today because of the choices I made yesterday.

* * *

We have to face the fact that either all of us are going to die together or we are going to learn to live together, and if we are to live together, we have to talk.

* * *

Will people ever be wise enough to refuse to follow bad leaders or to take away the freedom of other people?

* * *

If you can develop this ability to see what you look at, to understand its meaning, to readjust your knowledge to this new information, you can continue to learn and to grow as long as you live and you'll have a wonderful time doing it.

* * *

Be confident, not certain.

* * *

He who learns but does not think is lost. He who thinks but does not learn is in great danger.

* * *

It takes as much energy to wish as it does to plan.

* * *

Life must be lived, and curiosity kept alive. One must never, for whatever reason, turn his back on life.

* * *

When you cease to make a contribution, you begin to die.

* * *

It is not more vacation we need – it is more vocation.

* * *

Life is what you make it. Always has been, always will be.

JOHN KENNEDY

John Kennedy (May 29, 1917 – November 22, 1963) - was an American statesman who served as the 35th President of the United States.

* * *

Change is the law of life.
And those who look only to the past or present
are certain to miss the future.

* * *

As we express our gratitude,
we must never forget that the highest appreciation
is not to utter words, but to live by them.

* * *

The goal of education is the advancement of knowledge and
the dissemination of truth.

* * *

If we cannot now end our differences,
at least we can help make the world safe for diversity.

* * *

Physical fitness is not only one of the most important keys to
a healthy body, it is the basis of dynamic
and creative intellectual activity.

* * *

Efforts and courage are not enough
without purpose and direction.

* * *

Things do not happen.
Things are made to happen.

* * *

Forgive your enemies, but never forget their names.

* * *

Man is still the most extraordinary computer of all.

* * *

There are risks and costs to action.
But they are far less than the long-range risks of comfortable
inaction.

* * *

Mankind must put an end to war
before war puts an end to mankind.

* * *

Those who make peaceful revolution impossible
will make violent revolution inevitable.

* * *

Victory has a thousand fathers,
but defeat is an orphan.

CONNIE PODESTA

Connie Podesta (born 1975) Expert on High Performance, Leadership, Managing Change, Sales, and Communications.

* * *

I want to tell you something, women: Men aren't afraid of death, disease, torture or war. You know what wakes a man up in the middle of the night? In a cold sweat, the very thought that tomorrow, the very thought that tomorrow you will have him involved in a discussion about the relationship.

* * *

Standing out in a positive way isn't something you do some of the time. It's something you strive for all the time. Your social media should reflect that.

* * *

Difficult people are great actors. Every difficult person in your life – will you see them for what they are? Don't take it personally. It isn't about you. They treat their spouse this way... Difficult people have an act. And they either use their whining crying to make you feel guilty, so that you'll give in, or they use anger to make you afraid so that you will give in. Difficult people want one thing – they want their own way.

* * *

Powerful motivational speaking is so much more than smart words and a polished delivery; it is that ability to reach inside the audience and touch their minds, hearts, and souls so they will truly want to experience outstanding results in every area of their life – both work and home.

* * *

Healthy relationships are based on one thing – healthy communication, otherwise known as assertive, or to get right to the point – adult communication.

* * *

I am choosing to be more creative, more passionate, more productive, and more confident than ever before. Why? Because I have no other choice if I want to succeed. And, believe me, success is not an option for me; and hopefully, not for you either. Ready to tackle the world? Then start with a change and a choice. Change any attitudes and behaviors that may get in your way and sabotage your success. And choose to forge ahead with spirit, determination and a lot of love along the way.

* * *

Sometimes in our attempt to give children what we did not have, we forget to give our children what we did have.

* * *

The number 1 reason why someone has an affair in marriage is not about sex. It's because they no longer felt good about themselves in the presence of their spouse. The number 1 reason why an employee quits their job is not about money, it's because they no longer felt good about themselves in the presence of their management team. Ladies and gentleman, we make choices based on how we feel about ourselves.

* * *

The game of life is basically about getting our needs met.

* * *

Fairness isn't a given. Watch out for the warning signs and choose to surround yourself with people who play fair, work fair and live life with integrity.

* * *

Too often people let the past be about regrets and the future be about worry. Neither emotion is going to get your needs met, make you a better person, increase your ability to love and be loved, mend a heart, or solve a problem... at this moment.

* * *

The way we communicate is changing at lightning speed. If you want to out-think, out-perform the competition and be valued, you've got to change with it.

* * *

Women, shame on you! Don't you ever ask a man in your life again about your weight? You have a scale – get on it!

* * *

Difficult people have been trained and taught to act the way they do since they were children. In fact, they have been rewarded for their negative behavior throughout their entire lives. Difficult behavior worked for them as children, and more importantly, it continues to work for them as adults.

* * *

There's enough negative in the world to go around. My goals mirror those of most top leaders. People need real positive change today. They need to see possibilities where others see obstacles. They need to feel empowered rather than powerless. And they need real-world solutions to help them achieve these things. That's what I can bring to the table.

* * *

We are not attracted to people because of their strengths, we are attracted to people because of our weaknesses. Which is why it is so important that you understand yourself.

* * *

Change is what makes life exciting, daring, different, inspired. Stop fighting it. Embrace it!

* * *

If you don't understand people – customers, colleagues, leaders, owners, family, friends and yourself, there is NO WAY you can ever experience success – at any level

* * *

You are not your past. And your future? Will take care of itself – if you choose to live.

* * *

Indifferent and apathetic people are just as dangerous to your life as negative people. Apathy is contagious!

* * *

Men are so much better getting their needs met... If a guy has a need, he goes after it. Doesn't worry about it, doesn't feel guilty about it, he just moves on, gets it met, goes to the next step... Women, we have come so far. Professionally. We have broken every glass ceiling there is to break. We are CEOs of major companies, women are coaches of major sports teams, we are prime ministers of countries. Yet, do you know that the average woman today is no better at getting her personal needs met than she was a hundred years ago?

* * *

Communication is one of the most vital tools we can harness in terms of building better companies and better relationships. How you present yourself in person and now through social media platforms speaks volumes to your character, integrity and frankly, they are deciding factors for people to determine whether they want to do business with you.

* * *

Memories can either make you or break you. They can drag you down, destroy your confidence, wear out your spirit and keep you living in what was and not what is. Or they can be the foundation for unbelievable learning, new experiences, and a purposeful, happy life built on what you are capable of achieving at this very moment in time. Don't live in the past – learn from it.

* * *

Happiness is understanding that abundance is yours for the taking.

* * *

Procrastination? Career-killer. Joy-spoiler. Relationship-ender. Don't wait for tomorrow to be happier and more successful.

ALEXANDER THE GREAT

Alexander The Great (20/21 July 356 BC – 10/11 June 323 BC) - was a king of the Ancient Greek kingdom of Macedon and a member of the Argead dynasty.

* * *

There is nothing impossible to him who will try.

* * *

I am indebted to my father for living,
but to my teacher for living well.

* * *

I do not pilfer victory.

* * *

Remember upon the conduct of each
depends on the fate of all.

* * *

For my own part, I would rather excel in knowledge
of the highest secrets of philosophy than in arms.

* * *

My father will anticipate everything. He will leave you and me no chance to do a great and brilliant deed.

* * *

A tomb now suffices him for whom the whole world was not sufficient.

* * *

Whatever possession we gain by our sword cannot be sure or lasting, but the love gained by kindness and moderation is certain and durable.

* * *

I am not afraid of an army of lions led by a sheep; I am afraid of an army of sheep led by a lion.

HILLARY CLINTON

Hillary Clinton (born October 26, 1947) - one of the world's most dynamic and powerful living women, Clinton bided her time as First Lady of the United States during her husband, Bill Clinton's, presidency from 1993 to 2001, before commencing her own political career.

* * *

If a country doesn't recognize minority rights and human rights, including women's rights, you will not have the kind of stability and prosperity that is possible.

* * *

Women are the largest untapped reservoir of talent in the world.

* * *

I think the world would be a lot better off if more people were to define themselves in terms of their own standards and values and not what other people said or thought about them.

* * *

Do all the good you can, at all the times you can, to all the people you can, as long as ever you can.

* * *

Let's continue to stand up for those who are vulnerable to being left out or marginalized.

* * *

I believe that the rights of women and girls are the unfinished business of the 21st century. The worst thing that can happen in a democracy — as well as in an individual's life is to become cynical about the future and lose hope.

* * *

Human rights are women's rights, and women's rights are human rights.

* * *

I can't stand whining. I can't stand the kind of paralysis that some people fall into because they're not happy with the choices they've made. You live in a time when there are endless choices. ... But you have to work on yourself. ... Do something!

* * *

There is a sense that things if you keep positive and optimistic about what can be done, do work out.

* * *

Dignity does not come from avenging insults, especially from the violence that can never be justified. It comes from taking responsibility and advancing our common humanity.

* * *

I think that if you live long enough, you realize that so much of what happens in life is out of your control, but how you respond to it is in your control. That's what I try to remember.

* * *

We should remember that just as a positive outlook on life can promote good health, so can everyday acts of kindness.

* * *

You know, everybody has setbacks in their life, and everybody falls short of whatever goals they might set for themselves. That's part of living and coming to terms with who you are as a person.

* * *

If you want to know how strong a country's health system is, look at the well beings of its mothers.

* * *

Take criticism seriously, but not personally. If there is truth or merit in the criticism, try to learn from it. Otherwise, let it roll right off you.

JULIA CHILD

Julia Child (August 15, 1912 - August 13, 2004) was an American chef, author, and television personality. She is recognized for bringing French cuisine to the American public with her debut cookbook "Mastering the Art of French Cooking" and her subsequent television programs.

* * *

How can a nation be called great if its bread tastes like Kleenex?

* * *

You find yourself refreshed by the presence of cheerful people. Why not make an honest effort to confer that pleasure on others? Half the battle is gained if you never allow yourself to say anything gloomy.

* * *

Noncooks think it's silly to invest two hours' work in two minutes' enjoyment; but if cooking is evanescent, so is the ballet.

* * *

Life itself is the proper binge.

* * *

Personally, I don't think pure vegetarianism is a healthy lifestyle. I've often wondered to myself: Does a vegetarian look forward to dinner, ever?

* * *

Moderation. Small helpings. Sample a little bit of everything. These are the secrets of happiness and good health.

* * *

If you're in a good profession, it's hard to get bored, because you're never finished. There will always be work you haven't done.

* * *

Find something you're passionate about and keep tremendously interested in it.

* * *

The measure of achievement is not winning awards. It's doing something that you appreciate, something you believe is worthwhile. I think of my strawberry souffle. I did that at least 28 times before I finally conquered it.

* * *

Drama is very important in life: You have to come on with a bang! You never want to go out with a whimper.

* * *

I enjoy cooking with wine, sometimes I even put it in the food I'm cooking.

* * *

Dining with one's friends and beloved family is certainly one of life's primal and most innocent delights, one that is both soul-satisfying and eternal.

* * *

Always start out with a larger pot than what you think you need.

* * *

Celebrity has its uses. I can always get a seat in any restaurant.

* * *

I find that if I just taste everything and eat small portions, I maintain my weight. I watch my fat intake, but I eat hearty.

* * *

Tears mess up your make-up.

* * *

Remember, no one's more important than people! In other words, friendship is the most important thing. Not a career or housework, or one's fatigue; and it needs to be tended and nurtured.

* * *

In department stores, so much kitchen equipment is bought indiscriminately by people who just come in for men's underwear.

* * *

Fat gives things flavor.

* * *

Just like becoming an expert in wine – you learn by drinking it, the best you can afford – you learn about great food by finding the best there is, whether simply or luxurious. Then you savor it, analyze it, and discuss it with your companions, and you compare it with other experiences.

* * *

I was 32 when I started cooking; up until then, I just ate.

* * *

Some people like to paint pictures, or do gardening, or build a boat in the basement. Other people get a tremendous pleasure out of the kitchen because cooking is just as creative and imaginative an activity as drawing, or wood carving, or music.

* * *

In France, cooking is a serious art form and a national sport.

* * *

The secret of a happy marriage is finding the right person. You know they're right if you love to be with them all of the time.

* * *

You'll never know everything about anything, especially something you love.

* * *

You don't have to cook fancy or complicated masterpieces – just good food from fresh ingredients.

* * *

The only time to eat diet food is while you're waiting for the steak to cook.

* * *

In spite of food fads, fitness programs, and health concerns, we must never lose sight of a beautifully conceived meal.

* * *

Being tall is an advantage, especially in business. People will always remember you. And if you're in a crowd, you'll always have some clean air to breathe.

* * *

No one is born a great cook, one learns by doing.

* * *

It's fun to get together and have something good to eat at least once a day. That's what human life is all about – enjoying things.

If you're afraid of butter, use cream.

* * *

This is my invariable advice to people: Learn how to cook, try new recipes, learn from your mistakes, be fearless, and above all – have fun!

* * *

Noelle cuisine is so beautifully arranged on the plate – you know someone's fingers have been all over it.

* * *

The best way to execute French cooking is to get good and loaded and whack the hell out of a chicken. Bon appetite.

* * *

I think every woman should have a blowtorch.

* * *

I don't think about whether people will remember me or not. I've been an okay person. I've learned a lot. I've taught people a thing or two. That's what's important.

A cookbook is only as good as its worst recipe.

* * *

Always remember: If you're alone in the kitchen and you drop the lamb, you can always just pick it up. Who's going to know?

I just hate health food.

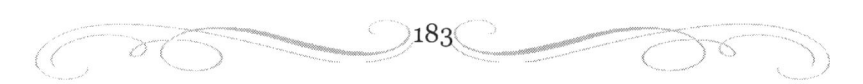

LAO TZU

Lao Tzu - was an ancient Chinese philosopher and writer. He is known as the reputed author of the "Tao Te Ching," the founder of philosophical Taoism.

* * *

Nature does not hurry,
yet everything is accomplished.

* * *

When I let go of what I am,
I become what I might be.

* * *

A good traveler has no fixed plans
and is not intent on arriving.

* * *

Life is a series of natural and spontaneous changes. Don't resist them; that only creates sorrow. Let reality be a reality. Let things flow naturally forward in whatever way they like.

* * *

Those who know do not speak. Those who speak do not know.

* * *

Those who are unaware they are walking in darkness will never see the light.

* * *

When you are content to be simply yourself and don't compare or compete, everyone will respect you.

* * *

The truth is not always beautiful, nor beautiful words the truth.

* * *

The best fighter is never angry.

* * *

Time is a created thing. To say 'I don't have time,' is like saying, 'I don't want to.

* * *

Because one believes in oneself,
one doesn't try to convince others.
Because one is content with oneself,
one doesn't need others' approval.
Because one accepts oneself,
the whole world accepts him or her.

* * *

A man with outward courage dares to die;
a man with inner courage dares to live.

ELIZABETH ARDEN

Elizabeth Arden (December 31, 1884 - October 18, 1966) was the founder, owner, and operator of Elizabeth Arden, Inc., a cosmetics and beauty corporation.

* * *

It was the beginning of my real life, my coming of age...

* * *

I vowed myself then and there to nature...

* * *

I... have been happy ever since.

* * *

Every skin requires an astringent tonic and a nourishing cream.

* * *

Keep it exquisitely clean.

* * *

Learn not to over-massage...

* * *

No one method of treatment sets the same with all persons...

* * *

Quest of the beautiful.

* * *

This business is... essentially feminine. What male executive will throw away a whole batch of powder, because the shade's off an indiscernible fraction? Or spend weeks mixing nail polish to get the right color – the one women will adore? I've been doing it every day of my life.

Everybody copies me.

* * *

I'm not interested in age. People who tell me their age are silly. You're as old as you feel.

* * *

Hold fast to life and youth.

* * *

Nothing that costs only a dollar is worth having.

* * *

Repetition makes reputation and reputation make customers.

* * *

I don't want them [staff] to love me, I want them to fear me.

* * *

[On the 1929 Wall Street Crash] Our clients are coping with the stress of financial loss by soaking in a hot bath scented with my Rose Geranium bath crystals.

* * *

I found I didn't really like looking at sick people. I want to keep people well, and young, and beautiful.

* * *

[In 1959 when she was told one of her racehorses had bitten off the tip of a person's finger] What happened to the horse?

* * *

[On passing by a limestone façade bearing the words 'Helena Rubinstein' after she had passed three weeks earlier at the age of 94] Poor Helena. [Elizabeth herself passed away just 18 months later at the age of 81]

* * *

When people think pink… they think Arden.

* * *

[At a political fundraiser towards the end of the 1930s] You don't have to do anything, my dears – just vote Republican.

* * *

[During the depression] Women are cheered by makeup. When the moneyed spend less on clothes, they spend more on lipstick.

* * *

Do you want your makeup to stay on for hours and hours?

* * *

Do you want something that will help keep a blemish out of sight?

* * *

Do you want your skin to glow through your powder?

* * *

Do you want to help hide your freckles?

* * *

You're in another world... when you come through the red door of Elizabeth Arden. And the world is based on one exclusive object – you. Whatever your need or the time you have on your hands.

* * *

[To her skeptical father] I am going to make us rich just as soon as I perfect my beauty cream.

* * *

Before you start off anything, why don't you start of with a clean slate.

* * *

Beautiful gives her daughter something to look forward to.

* * *

Beautiful stands the test of time.

* * *

Beautiful is knowing you are one of a kind.

* * *

Beautiful never looks back.

* * *

Some people feel the rain. Others just get wet.

Be true to who you are.

Beautiful blossoms in every season.

* * *

I rarely hire anyone who is out of a job.

* * *

I pick good women, but I haven't had any luck with my men. [On Helena Rubinstein] That woman.

* * *

[On reading 'Elizabeth and Her German Garden' – It] Brought back my childhood with a rush and all the happy days I spent in a garden… It was the beginning of my real life, my coming of age as it were, and entering into my kingdom… I vowed myself then and there to nature, and have been happy ever since.

* * *

To have a wholesome skin is to keep it exquisitely clean. Many times the skin is not thoroughly cleaned, and this is the real cause of blackheads and an impure complexion. It must be light and very oily to properly remove all impurities and prevent the pores from becoming clogged.

* * *

My long experience and great success have positively convinced me that every skin requires an astringent tonic and a nourishing cream.

* * *

Woman has always been searching for the Fountain of Youth, when, like the 'Blue Bird,' it is at home, and simply means ten minutes care night and morning.

* * *

To have a wholesome skin is to keep it exquisitely clean. Many times, the skin is not thoroughly cleaned, and this is the real cause of blackheads and an impure complexion. It must be light and very oily to properly remove all impurities and prevent the pores from becoming clogged.

* * *

It is equally important to promote and stimulate the circulation and clear and firm the skin.

* * *

Learn not to over-massage the face which gives a lifeless looking skin.

* * *

A wholesome, healthy skin, if wrongly treated can become gradually shriveled, old and haggard.

* * *

The very best treatment for the face and throat is to firm the lines and muscles by a peculiar patting in of…

* * *

[On Venetian Special Herb Astringent Cream] This particularly potent astringent firms as if by magic.

* * *

Be taught to administer this treatment yourself. It is well worth learning how.

* * *

The great lesson to learn about beauty charms is that no one method of treatment sets the same with all persons.

* * *

[On Venetian Powder V'illusion] A fascinating shade for sunburned faces.

* * *

Prepare your skin for July and August...

* * *

Beauty treatment is not complete without lipstick.

* * *

There's only one Elizabeth like me, and that's the Queen.

* * *

Go out and make your mark.

* * *

[To her husband (later ex-husband)] Dear, never forget one little point. It's my business. You just work here.

* * *

Women invented management.

* * *

Every woman has a right to be beautiful.

* * *

A woman can always look younger than she really is.

* * *

[The single-minded goal that drove her] To be the richest little woman in the world.

* * *

I only want people around me who can do the impossible.

* * *

Standards should be set by me and not imposed on me.

* * *

To be beautiful is the birthright of every woman.

* * *

It is remarkable what a woman can accomplish with just a little ambition.

* * *

To achieve beauty, a woman must first achieve health.

* * *

A beautiful horse is like a beautiful woman.

* * *

You're as old as you feel.

* * *

I want them to fear me.

* * *

The cosmetics industry is the nastiest business in the world.

I am going to make us rich...

* * *

Woman has always been searching for the Fountain of Youth...

* * *

Do not produce an artificial, unnatural look by doing too much to your skin.

* * *

The quest of the beautiful.

Beauty is one-part nature, and three parts care.

* * *

There is no reason for a woman to lose even one iota of her beauty.

* * *

There are only three American names that are known in every corner of the globe: Singer sewing machines, Coca-Cola and Elizabeth Arden.

* * *

To have a wholesome skin is to keep it exquisitely clean.

* * *

This business is… essentially feminine.

* * *

What male executive will throw away a whole batch of powder, because the shade's off an indiscernible fraction?

* * *

I'm not interested in age.

* * *

People who tell me their age are silly.

* * *

Many times, the skin is not thoroughly cleaned, and this is the real cause of blackheads and an impure complexion.

* * *

I didn't really like looking at sick people.

* * *

I want to keep people well, and young, and beautiful.

* * *

A woman must first achieve health.

* * *

Women are cheered by makeup.

* * *

When the moneyed spend less on clothes, they spend more on lipstick.

You're in another world...

* * *

Why don't you start off with a clean slate?

* * *

Many women today still have these same old-fashioned postures.

* * *

Your posture can be made perfect.

* * *

All the happy days I spent in a garden.

GLORIA STEINEM

Gloria Steinem (born March 25, 1934) is an American feminist, journalist, and social-political activist who became nationally recognized as a leader and a spokeswoman for the American feminist movement in the late 1960s and early 1970s.

* * *

A woman reading Playboy feels a little like a Jew reading a Nazi manual.

* * *

The truth will set you free, but first, it will piss you off.

* * *

Any woman who chooses to behave like a full human being should be warned that the armies of the status quo will treat her as something of a dirty joke. That's their natural and first weapon. She will need her sisterhood.

* * *

I have yet to hear a man ask for advice on how to combine marriage and a career.

* * *

Far too many people are looking for the right person, instead of trying to be the right person.

* * *

A feminist is anyone who recognizes the equality and full humanity of women and men.

* * *

If women are supposed to be less rational and more emotional at the beginning of our menstrual cycle when the female hormone is at its lowest level, then why isn't it logical to say that, in those few days, women behave the most like the way men behave all month long?

* * *

A woman without a man is like a fish without a bicycle.

* * *

Once we give up searching for approval, we often find it easier to earn respect.

* * *

We'll never solve the feminization of power until we solve the masculinity of wealth.

* * *

Marriage: A ceremony in which rings are put on the finger of the lady and through the nose of the gentleman.

* * *

Planning ahead is a measure of class. The rich and even the middle-class plan for future generations, but the poor can plan ahead only a few weeks or days.

* * *

Women have two choices: Either she's a feminist or a masochist.

* * *

We've begun to raise daughters more like sons… but few have the courage to raise our sons more like our daughters.

* * *

The first problem for all of us, men and women, is not to learn, but to unlearn.

There are really not many jobs that actually require a penis or a vagina, and all other occupations should be open to everyone.

* * *

One day an army of gray-haired women may quietly take over the Earth.

* * *

God may be in the details, but the goddess is in the questions. Once we begin to ask them, there's no turning back.

* * *

Marriage works best for men than women. The two happiest groups are married men and unmarried women.

* * *

Most American children suffer too much mother and too little father.

* * *

No man can call himself liberal, or radical, or even a conservative advocate of fair play, if his work depends in any way on the unpaid or underpaid labor of women at home, or in the office.

Clearly, no one knows what leadership has gone undiscovered in women of all races, and in black and other minority men.

* * *

From pacifist to terrorist, each person condemns violence – and then adds one cherished case in which it may be justified

* * *

Most women are one man away from welfare.

* * *

Someone asked me why women don't gamble as much as men do, and I gave the commonsensical reply that we don't have as much money. That was a true and incomplete answer. In fact, women's total instinct for gambling is satisfied by marriage.

* * *

Hope is a very unruly emotion.

* * *

Women may be the one group that grows more radical with age.

* * *

Without leaps of imagination or dreaming, we lose the excitement of possibilities. Dreaming, after all, is a form of planning.

* * *

Most women's magazines simply try to mold women into bigger and better consumers.

* * *

Self-esteem isn't everything; it's just that there's nothing without it.

* * *

Law and justice are not always the same. When they aren't, destroying the law may be the first step toward changing it.

* * *

A woman who aspires to be something is called a bitch.

* * *

Men should think twice before making widowhood women's only path to power.

* * *

This is no simple reform. It really is a revolution. Sex and race because they are easy and visible differences have been the primary ways of organizing human beings into superior and inferior groups and into the cheap labor on which this system still depends. We are talking about a society in which there will be no roles other than those chosen or those earned. We are really talking about humanism.

* * *

We are the women our parents warned us against, and we are proud.

* * *

The authority of any governing institution must stop at its citizen's skin.

* * *

America is an enormous frosted cupcake in the middle of millions of starving people.

* * *

If the shoe doesn't fit, must we change the foot?

* * *

Feminism has never been about getting a job for one woman. It's about making life more fair for women everywhere. It's not about a piece of the existing pie; there are too many of us for that. It's about baking a new pie.

* * *

I have yet to hear a man ask for advice on how to combine marriage and a career.

* * *

But the problem is that when I go around and speak on campuses, I still don't get young men standing up and saying, how can I combine career and family?

* * *

I always wanted to be a writer. I got into activism just because it needed to be done.

* * *

Childbirth is more admirable than conquest, more amazing than self-defense, and as courageous as either one.

* * *

Don't worry about what you should do, worry about what you can do. Writing is the only thing that when I do it, I don't feel I should be doing something else.

* * *

The family is the basic cell of government: it is where we are trained to believe that we are human beings or that we are chattel, it is where we are trained to see the sex and race divisions and become callous to injustice even if it is done to ourselves, to accept as biological a full system of authoritarian government.

* * *

Pornography is the instruction. Rape is the practice, battered women are the practice, and battered children are the practice.

* * *

The first resistance to social change is to say it's not necessary.

* * *

I have met brave women who are exploring the outer edge of possibility, with no history to guide them and courage to make themselves vulnerable that I find moving beyond the words to express it.

* * *

Women are always saying, We can do anything that men can do. But Men should be saying, We can do anything that women can do.

* * *

Rich people plan for three generations. Poor people plan for Saturday night.

* * *

A pedestal is as much a prison as any small, confined space.

* * *

Power can be taken, but not given. The process of the taking is empowerment in itself.

* * *

For women... bras, panties, bathing suits, and other stereotypical gear are visual reminders of a commercial, idealized feminine image that our real and diverse female bodies can't possibly fit. Without these visual references, each individual woman's body demands to be accepted on its own terms. We stop being comparatives. We begin to be unique.

* * *

We can tell our values by looking at our checkbook stubs.

It is more rewarding to watch money change the world than watch it accumulate.

* * *

However sugarcoated and ambiguous, every form of authoritarianism must start with a belief in some group's greater right to power, whether that right is justified by sex, race, class, religion or all four. However far it may expand, the progression inevitably rests on unequal power and airtight roles within the family

* * *

The future depends entirely on what each of us does every day; a movement is only people moving.

* * *

So whatever you want to do, just do it… making a damn fool of yourself is absolutely essential.

* * *

A liberated woman is one who has sex before marriage and a job after.

Women are not going to be equal outside the home until men are equal in it.

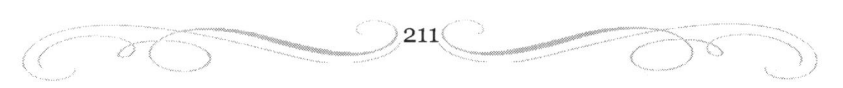

HENRY FORD

Henry Ford (July 30, 1863 – April 7, 1947) - was an American captain of industry and a business magnate, the founder of the Ford Motor Company, and the sponsor of the development of the assembly line technique of mass production.

* * *

You can't build a reputation
on what you are going to do.

* * *

Employers only handle the money.
It is the customer who pays the wages.

* * *

If there is any one secret of success, it lies in the ability to get
the other person's point of view
and see things from that person's angle
as well as from your own.

* * *

Thinking is the hardest work there is,
which is probably the reason, so few engage in it.

* * *

You don't have to hold a position
in order to be a leader.

* * *

Failure is simply the opportunity to begin again,
this time more intelligently.

* * *

As we advance in life
we learn the limits of our abilities.

* * *

Enthusiasm is the yeast
that makes your hopes shine to the stars.

* * *

I do not believe a man can ever leave his business.
He ought to think of it by day and dream
of it by night.

* * *

Quality means doing it right when no one is looking.

* * *

One of the greatest discoveries a man makes,
one of his great surprises, is to find he can do what he was
afraid he couldn't do.

* * *

Vision without execution is just hallucination.

* * *

I believe God is managing affairs
and that He doesn't need any advice from me.
With God in charge, I believe everything will
work out for the best in the end.
So, what is there to worry about.

* * *

There is one rule for the industrialist, and that is: make the best quality goods possible at the lowest cost possible, paying the highest wages possible.

* * *

To do more for the world than the world
does for you that is success.

* * *

The highest use of capital is not to make more money, but to make money do more for the betterment of life.

* * *

There is no man living
who isn't capable of doing more
then he thinks he can do.

SALLY KRISTEN RIDE

Sally Kristen Ride (May 26, 1951 – July 23, 2012) was an American astronaut, physicist, and engineer. Born in Los Angeles, she joined NASA in 1978 and became the first American woman in space in 1983.

* * *

The stars don't look bigger, but they do look brighter.

* * *

When you're getting ready to launch into space, you're sitting on a big explosion just waiting to happen.

* * *

I've discovered that half the people would love to go into space and there's no need to explain it to them. The other half can't understand, and I couldn't explain it to them. If someone doesn't know why I can't explain it.

* * *

All adventures—especially into new territory—are scary.

* * *

I think there probably is life, maybe primitive life, in outer space. There might be very primitive life in our solar system — single-cell animals, that sort of thing.

* * *

The stars don't look bigger, but they do look brighter.

* * *

Studying whether there's life on Mars or studying how the universe began, there's something magical about pushing back the frontiers of knowledge.

* * *

I suggest taking the high road and have a little sense of humor and let things roll off your back.

* * *

Suppose you came across a woman lying on the street with an elephant sitting on her chest. You notice she is short of breath. Shortness of breath can be a symptom of heart problems. In her case, the much more likely cause is the elephant on her chest. For a long time, society put obstacles in the way of women who wanted to enter the sciences. That is the elephant.

* * *

If we want scientists and engineers in the future, we should be cultivating the girls as much as the boys.

* * *

The view of earth is absolutely spectacular, and the feeling of looking back and seeing your planet as a planet is just an amazing feeling. It's a totally different perspective, and it makes you appreciate, actually, how fragile our existence is.

* * *

I have been a bit of a risk taker all my life.

* * *

If I think I've accomplished what I set out to accomplish, then that's achievement.

* * *

Try to understand who you are and what you want to do, and don't be afraid to go down that road and do whatever it takes and work as hard as you have to work to achieve that.

* * *

It's also critical to prepare the core of the future skilled workforce. That's because in the next decade or so, fully 80 of the jobs in this country, that includes basic living wage jobs, are going to require some background in science, math or technology.

* * *

Women and men go through exactly the same jobs on orbit. Weightlessness is a great equalizer.

* * *

I never went into physics or the astronaut corps to become a role model. But after my first flight, it became clear to me that I was one.

* * *

I'm not a goal-oriented person. I don't look out into the future and say, 'Five or ten years from now, this is what I want to be doing, this is where I want to be.' I'm very much a person who gets very, very involved in whatever I happen to be doing now.

OSCAR WILDE

Oscar Wilde
(16 October 1854 – 30 November 1900)
- was an Irish writer.
He wrote plays, fiction, essays, and poetry.

* * *

Success is a science; if you have the conditions, you get the result.

* * *

Experience is simply the name we give our mistakes.

* * *

True friends stab you in the front.

* * *

Women are made to be loved, not understood.

* * *

Always forgive your enemies,
nothing annoys them so much.

* * *

I am so clever that sometimes I don't understand
a single word of what I am saying.

* * *

Most people are other people.
Their thoughts are someone else's opinions,
their lives a mimicry, their passions a quotation.

* * *

Morality is simply the attitude
we adopt towards people
whom we personally dislike.

* * *

Dividing people into good and bad is absurd.
People are either charming or tedious.

* * *

The only thing to do with good advice
is to pass it on. It is never of any use to oneself.

* * *

Nothing can cure the soul but the senses,
just as nothing can cure the senses but the soul.

* * *

I am not young enough to know everything.

* * *

A man who does not think for himself does not think at all.

JOAN RIVERS

Joan Alexandra Molinsky, known professionally as Joan Rivers (June 8, 1933 – September 4, 2014), was an American comedian, actress, writer, producer, and television host.

* * *

I bought a pedigree dog for 300$. My friend said, give me 300$, and I'll shit on your carpet.

* * *

I knew I was an unwanted baby when I saw that my bath toys were a toaster and a radio.

* * *

I once dated a guy who was so dumb, he couldn't count to twenty-one unless he was naked.

* * *

He said I don't want to wake you up.

* * *

I'm Jewish. I don't work out. If God wanted us to bend over, he'd put diamonds on the floor.

* * *

I have so little sex appeal my gynecologist calls me sir.

* * *

The first time I see a jogger smiling, I'll consider it.

* * *

Don't cook. Don't clean. No man will ever make love to a woman because she waxed the linoleum. My God, the floor's immaculate! Lie down, you hot bitch.

* * *

Mick Jagger could French-kiss a moose. He has child-bearing lips.

* * *

Madonna is so hairy – when she lifted her arm, I thought it was Tina Turner in her armpit.

* * *

All my mother told me about sex was that the man goes on top and the woman on the bottom. For three years my husband and I slept in bunk beds.

* * *

I said to my mother-in-law, my house is your house. She said, Get the hell of my property.

* * *

I was so flat I used to put Xs on my chest and write, You are here. I wore angora sweaters just so the guys would have something to pet.

* * *

I said to my husband, my boobs have gone, my stomach's gone, say something nice about my legs. He said Blue goes with everything.

* * *

It's been so long since I made love, I can't remember who gets tied up.

* * *

I like colonic irrigation because sometimes you find old jewelry.

* * *

When a man has a birthday, he takes a day off. When a woman has a birthday, she takes at least three years off.

* * *

Is she fat? Her favorite food is seconds.

* * *

– Come on, Joan, tell us which husband was the best lover?
– Yours. – Joan Rivers, Joan Collins

* * *

I hate housework. You make the beds, you do the dishes, and six months later, you have to start all over again.

* * *

The only time a woman has a true orgasm is when she is shopping.

* * *

Anger is a symptom, a way of cloaking and expressing feelings too awful to experience directly – hurt, bitterness, grief and, most of all, fear.

* * *

The nice thing about Viagra is that they are proving men can go blind on it, so you can gain weight and have a great sex life.

* * *

I was the last girl in Larchmont, NY to get married. My mother had a sign up Last Girl Before Freeway.

* * *

My sex life is so bad, my G-spot has been declared a historical landmark.

* * *

When I saw her sex tape, all I could think of were Paris Hilton's poor parents. The shame, the shame of the Hilton family. To have your daughter do a porno film… in a Marriott hotel.

* * *

I met Adele! What's her song, Rolling in The Deep? She should add fried chicken.

* * *

Don't cook. Don't clean. No man will ever make love to a woman because she waxed the Linoleum. My God, the floor's immaculate! Lie down, you hot bitch.

* * *

No man ever stuck his hand up your dress looking for a library ticket.

* * *

I wish I had a twin so I could know what I'd look like without plastic surgery.

* * *

My daughter and I are very close. We speak every single day, and I call her every day, and I say the same thing, Pick up, I know you're there. And she says the same thing back, How'd you get this new number?

* * *

A friend of mine confused her Valium with her birth control pills. She had 14 kids but didn't give a shit.

* * *

Taking advice about marriage from Elizabeth Taylor is like taking sailing lessons from the captain of the Titanic.

* * *

I was dating a transvestite. My mother said, Marry him. You'll double your wardrobe.

* * *

I have so little sex appeal my gynecologist examines me by telephone.

* * *

A man can sleep around, no questions asked. But if a woman makes 19 or 20 mistakes, she's a tramp.

* * *

My love life is like a piece of Swiss cheese. Most of it's missing, and what's there stinks.

* * *

I've worked with Angelina Jolie. She saw a sign that said Wet Floor one time, and she did.

* * *

Don't tell your kids you had an easy birth or they won't respect you. For years I used to wake up my daughter and say, Melissa, you ripped me to shreds. Now go back to sleep.

* * *

My best birth control now is just to leave the lights on.

* * *

People say that money is not the key to happiness, but I always figured if you have enough money, you can have a key made.

* * *

Bo Derek is so stupid she returns bowling balls because they've got holes in them.

A child of one can be taught not to do certain things such as touch a hot stove, turn on the gas, pull lamps off their tables by their cords, or wake mommy before noon.

* * *

Thank God we're living in a country where the sky's the limit, the stores are open late and you can shop in bed thanks to television.

* * *

I was just reading about the new Lindsay Lohan diet, which is all liquid. 80 proof.

* * *

Elizabeth Taylor was so fat that whenever she went to London in a red dress, 30 passengers would try to board her.

* * *

I have no sex appeal, which kills me. The only way I can ever hear heavy breathing from my husband's side of the bed is when he's having an asthma attack.

* * *

You want to get Cindy Crawford confused? Ask her to spell mom backward.

* * *

When you first get married, they open the car door for you. Eighteen years now... once he opened the car door for me in the last four years – we were on the freeway at the time.

* * *

If Kate Winslet had dropped a few pounds, the Titanic would never have sunk.

* * *

The whole Michael Jackson thing was my fault. I told him to date only 28-year-olds. Who knew he would find 20 of them?

* * *

It takes a lot of experience for a girl to kiss like a beginner.

* * *

My face has been tucked in more times than a bedsheet at the Holiday Inn.

* * *

No-one says this, but the vagina drops. I looked down a few years ago and thought, why am I wearing a bunny slipper?

* * *

Don't talk to me about Valentine's Day. At my age, an affair of the heart is a bypass.!

* * *

I've had so much plastic surgery, when I die, they will donate my body to Tupperware.

* * *

I have no sex appeal. I have to blindfold my vibrator.

* * *

Two's company. Three's fifty bucks.

* * *

Trust your husband, adore your husband, and get as much as you can in your own name.

* * *

Marie Osmond is so pure, not even Moses could part her knees.

Made in the USA
Lexington, KY
29 July 2019